Who's the Boss?

The Integreship Group

Take charge • Trust yourself • Do great things

Karen Alber
Amy Ruppert
Rachel Schaming

Published by The Integreship_SM Group, LLC
332 S. Michigan Ave. Suite 1032 - 1243
Chicago, Illinois 60604-4434
312-967-5858

Authored by:
Karen Alber
Amy Ruppert
Rachel Schaming

Book cover, graphics and typesetting by Jason Brown of Mothlight Design
New Glarus, Wisconsin

Illustrations by Joe Giunta

Library of Congress Cataloging-in-Publication Data
The Integreship_SM Group, LLC
Who's the Boss? : Confront the Elephant in the Room

Includes bibliographical references in footnotes.

SUBJECT MATTER REGISTERED

Situations, characters and stories in this book are a work of fiction and are based
on common themes seen in the workplace. Names, characters, businesses, places,
events and incidents are either the products of the authors' imaginations or used
in a fictitious manner. Any resemblance to actual persons, living or dead, or actual
events is purely coincidental.

While the publisher and authors of this book have made every effort to provide
accurate information on third parties referenced in the book, neither the publisher
or authors assume any responsibility for errors, or for changes that occur after
publication.

About the Authors

Karen Alber

Amy Ruppert

Rachel Schaming

After 10 years in the C-suite as the CIO at MillerCoors and HJ Heinz, Karen made the decision to leave corporate life in order to focus on what was most important to her – family and making a difference. Karen is now helping other leaders and organizations drive change based on integrity, values and tough, but civil leadership.

Her many years working her way up from a shop floor supervisor to the C-suite in supply chain management and information technology underpins her work coaching individuals and organizations to enact positive change that becomes the way we work around here.

Considered one of the early pioneers in professional coaching and known as 'the coaches coach', Amy has led in several capacities to shape and form coaching to the thriving industry it is today.

On the ground floor in 1995 when the International Coach Federation (ICF) was formed, Amy contributed in several leadership roles since the industry began with under 200 professional coaches in North America to more than 20,000 in 110 countries today. She is also an ICF Master Certified Coach.

Amy has also maintained a private practice working with hundreds of high profile leaders since 1995, as well as working with dozens of organizations in establishing internal coaching initiatives.

A SHRM, SCP human resource executive with nearly three decades of experience in leading people, processes, systems and cultures in innovative change initiatives, Rachel left the corporate environment to offer leaders and organizations her many years of experience spanning high-tech, legal, healthcare and aerospace industries.

Her reputation in taming abrasive leaders and working with organizations to systematize integrity and values-based leadership is unmatched. Rachel has published more than 200 articles on these and other related topics and is a frequently requested speaker on organizational and leadership development topics.

This book is dedicated to the managers, supervisors, team leads, executives and senior leaders who strive to do the right thing and lead with integrity.

Contents

"We have written this book to open the conversation that few people want to have, yet everyone seems to need. We are taking on those power dynamics that can be tremendously complex and confusing. The tough stuff that can range from small miscommunications that cause hard feelings all the way to unethical or illegal actions."

"YOU are the boss of your choices, the steward of your values and the keeper of your integrity."

Normally congenial co-worker or boss begins to demonstrate erratic or unacceptable behavior.

Managing up to look good while disrespecting or dismissing others.

Abusing title and organizational role — unrealistic and inappropriate demands of others.

Unethical, illegal or out-of-policy conduct — visible to many and unaddressed.

Tools to help weigh out risks, options and rewards in order to be confident that whatever risk you take or don't take, is right for you given all the circumstances.

See the models and process in action relative to each of the four stories in chapters 2, 3, 4 and 5.

7 Strategies to focus on for greater resilience and building courage.

A review of key points in graphics.

The chapter title says it all.

Foreword

You are working closely with another manager who is territorial and passive-aggressive. Now what?

How many times have you heard yourself or someone you know anguish over complex power clashes like these? Seemingly no-win, soul-killing situations where the stakes are high and you could suffer grave consequences if you spoke up. How do you get to some sort of resolution? How do you advise, manage, mentor or coach someone else stuck in these situations?

There are scores of books and training programs about leadership development, yet very few that give any practical tools to navigate the confusion and frustration that come from these types of situations. **Who's the Boss?** hits right to the heart of these complex power dynamics and offers a proven and effective process to help you self-navigate or coach someone else to a resolution.

Written by three seasoned leaders; the former CIO of MillerCoors and HJ Heinz, a Human Resources executive with over 30 years of experience, and one of the early pioneers and leaders in the professional coaching field. This book reflects their collective wisdom and leadership experience that takes on some of the most challenging realities leaders face.

"Alber, Ruppert, and Schaming offer a sensible and usable guide to navigating and resolving some of the toughest but most ubiquitous challenges we all face in the workplace — what they call the "cringe moments." Using all too familiar case examples, they offer a clear framework for organizing our emotional responses and our risks and for crafting experience-tested scripts and action plans to resolve these challenges. They provide a playbook for not only "voicing our values," but doing so in ways that benefit ourselves, our colleagues and our organizations. Reading "Who's The Boss? Confront the Elephant in the Room" is empowering, enlightening, and energizing."

Mary C. Gentile, PhD

Author of "Giving Voice To Values: How To Speak Your Mind When You Know What's Right" (www.GivingVoiceToValuesTheBook.com)

"As a labor and employment lawyer with over 44 years experience in litigation and advising employers, I found this book fascinating in detailing the eternal struggle of dealing with people at work, whether they be peers, subordinates or "bosses." How one reacts to each of these interest groups determines how one gets along in the workplace. "Who's The Boss?" taps the collective experience of three highly successful professionals and is a must read for anyone dealing with conflict at work. Using vignettes to illustrate their points, the authors give us valuable information to "navigate" those "cringe moments" where we can either recoil or move forward with confidence. I particularly liked the acronym LEAD which is the roadmap to success in dealing with the difficult boss or peer. The strategies can be implemented by anyone with workplace issues. In most cases, it is not illegal to have a "jerk for a boss." However, it can lead to illegal conduct and it is also frustrating. This book bridges the knowledge gap from fear and hurt to constructive strategies and coping methods that will in large part, make your work life much more pleasant. I highly recommend this book to anyone dealing with conflict generally and workplace conflict specifically."

Thom K. Cope
Partner — Mesch, Clark, Rothschild
Author of "How Not to be a Stupid Manager"

Introduction

How many times have you heard yourself, a family member, friend, peer or loved one complain about the relationship they are experiencing with someone at work? How do you respond when you are stuck in a seemingly no-win situation that you have with your boss, a peer or your boss's boss? How do you advise, manage, mentor or coach someone stuck in these situations? With the infinite number of books written about leadership, very few of them provide the day-to-day practical tools to address the challenges and solve the sticky and often very complex situations of workplace power dynamics which occur in *every* workplace, *every* day.

> Your boss's peer, who also happens to be a good friend of your boss, misrepresents YOUR team's work. Now what?

This book is to show leaders at all levels who find themselves stuck without navigation tools in these types of power clashes how to get unstuck and find resolution. It's for those who find themselves in situations where they feel like they're selling a piece of their soul and would suffer grave consequences if they tried to reclaim it by speaking up.

> In order to look good, your boss asks you to present something you know is not accurate. Now what?

Our collective experience as senior corporate executives and as executive coaches has shown us some of the best in leadership, as well as some of the worst. One thing we know for certain is that these challenging to toxic power dynamics happen more frequently than anyone is comfortable talking about. So much, in fact, that recent metrics show some alarming trends in U.S. businesses that connect directly to these types of dynamics. A 2012 Gallup survey shows 7 out of 10 employees in the U.S. are disengaged from their work and their company, costing U.S. businesses about $500 billion per year.[1]

Leaders today find themselves having to strike a balance between the needs of stakeholders and the countless conflicting needs of their employees. The pressure of keeping people scores high and stakeholders happy requires managers to dance, almost flawlessly, through a gauntlet of competing priorities. This tension has set many leaders

> *You've been told to do something that borders on unethical behavior by a senior leader. Now what?*

up to fail miserably at being decent human beings. It often brings out the worst in good people and exacerbates character weaknesses. These are exactly the dynamics that erode engagement and trust throughout organizations.

---

1   Gallup Q12: State of the American Workplace: Employee Engagement Insights for U.S. Business Leaders

We have written this book to open the conversation few people really want to have, yet everyone seems to need. We are taking on those power dynamics that can be tremendously complex and confusing. The tough stuff that can range from small miscommunications that cause hard feelings all the way to unethical or even illegal situations. And there are millions of situations — amongst them contentious politics, bullying, veiled threats, conflict avoidance, mobbing, hostility and incivility to name a few, that fall throughout the power dynamic continuum and wreak havoc in teams, departments and entire organizations.

The authors of this book, and countless other leaders, have been there. We have been confronted with having to make a choice and face those personal moments of truth that either moved us towards or away from our integrity. With the challenging relationships you face in the workplace you may be questioning "who have I become" or "who will I become" if you continue down the same path of what Robert Frost calls a life of "quiet desperation". And understandably, we can get stuck there because there's too much at stake to change the situation and, in turn, we become paralyzed or disillusioned. It's a quiet suffering that affects our health, our relationships and our outlook.

> *Your manager rails at you about things you've done that you've seen her do a hundred times. You just can't take it anymore. Now what?*

This book will provide you with a practical approach and process for finding your way out of a seemingly "no win" situation or helping someone else in one. It will also give you strategies for building resilience to find courage and strength of character in order to do the right thing. We intend that this book will lead you to a solution that enhances and restores your relationship with the person or people you are challenged by without compromising your integrity.

When you hear all of the bad workplace relationship stories out there, it is easy to fall into hopeless cynicism about the state of leadership. We may watch the evening news and witness people with power acting with an overt self-interest and insatiable greed. We may go to work and experience a lack of respect from some of the leaders above us and some of the reports below us. We may also find ourselves sandwiched into situations that have us questioning who is right, what is right, and how we can find it within ourselves to do the right thing.

We are merely opening the conversation in this book, and we will continue the conversation with fresh learning from seasoned leaders in our work at The Integreship℠Group. We hope this is just the beginning of our relationship with you and that you'll join us in our mission to help leaders take charge, trust themselves and do great and wonderful things in the world.

Chapter 1

Who IS the Boss?

YOU are!

This core principle underlies everything you will read in this book.

YOU are the boss of YOU.

You are the Boss of your Choices.

You have a choice in how you respond to even the ugliest and most reprehensible situations. This is within your influence and control. The bullying boss, conniving counterpart and backstabbing peer have no jurisdiction over how *you* react and respond to what they have done or not done.

You are the Steward of your Values.

Regardless of our backgrounds, culture, gender or age, we all share common, universal values that are directly related to right and wrong. When we are faced with incivility or abusive behavior from someone we work with, one or more of these values is at play. Making choices to respond in ways that align with and preserve the value(s) at risk will make you a good steward of your values.

You are the Keeper of your Integrity.

Acting with integrity means what you say and do is aligned with your values. How that looks and is carried out is unique to every person. The mission of this book is designed to move you back into alignment with the values most affected by the situation you are facing.

Acting with Integrity Connects You with the Most Authentic Parts of You!

When you lose touch with knowing you are the boss of you, it's easy to slide into a victim mindset, often unknowingly. Once that happens, the notion that you have the power to change things can be erased. You may begin to shrink and give up more and more of your self as things escalate. You might question everything and become increasingly ungrounded, causing you to possibly hang on to threads of hope that things will get better eventually. Although you know you should do something, you may remain in the same place, fearing the repercussions of taking action. Acting with integrity means you are in touch with and utilizing the very best and most authentic parts of yourself. You are able to take charge, trust yourself and be the boss of YOU!

You Are Not Alone

The statistics are alarming. And so is the fallout.

> 80% of U.S. workers believe incivility is a problem in the workplace.
> 96% have experienced incivility themselves.
> 48% claim they are treated with incivility at least once a week.
> 75% are dissatisfied with how their company handles incivility.[2]

---

2   The Cost of Bad Behavior by Christine Pearson & Christine Porath

Rising rates of depression, anxiety and stress-related healthcare costs are reported each year. Researchers from Harvard and Stanford have reported:

- Job insecurity raises the odds of self-reported poor physical health by about 50 percent.
- Low organizational justice increases the odds of having a physician-diagnosed condition by about 50 percent.
- Adverse psycho-social situations at work, i.e., lack of fairness, low social support and low job control, were as strongly associated with poor health as factors such as shift work and long hours.
- Workplace stress contributes to at least 120,000 deaths each year (which parallels the annual number of accidental deaths in the U.S.) and accounts for up to $190 billion in healthcare costs.[3]

All of this points to a systemic leadership crisis in our workplaces.

What Relationships Are Suffering Most in the Workplace?

In this book we will use the word "Boss" as a common label for the troubled relationships we'll be focusing on, however, our definition of *Boss* includes anyone who has power or authority over you, your responsibilities and your career future. In today's organizations, we can have dotted line responsibilities to more than one leader in the company i.e., "multiple bosses" and interact with many others who have the

---

3   Workplace Stressors & Health Outcomes: Health policy for the workplace AND The Relationship Between Workplace Stressors and Mortality and Health Costs in the United States by Joel Goh, Jeffrey Pfeffer, & Stefanos A. Zenios

same or similar influence as the boss you report to directly. "The boss" can also be someone at your peer level (or slightly above) who has strategically placed themselves close to your boss or other leaders in the organization, and has their ear. And last, "the boss" can be the boss of your boss. The larger the organization, the more systemic and complex the boss relationships.

As the three authors of this book, our collective experience has been that most people with authority in companies are good people who want to do good by others. More often than not, most leaders come with positive intentions, and believe in compassion and have a strong moral foundation. When good leaders are thrust into extremely demanding and almost impossible situations such as litigious minefields, unrelenting shareholders demanding high returns, global competition and fierce wars for talent, all of this stress cascades to the next level. Good people are thrust into values conflicts and begin compromising who they really are and what they really believe, to meet the demands coming across their desks.

As the pressure increases for leaders, so does their inability to cover personality vulnerabilities and exaggerations. All of one's stored lifetime experiences imprinted on the psyche and one's learned belief systems get triggered and amplified when threatened. Each leader has a different threshold of tolerance as he/she moves towards survival mode and, once there, becomes someone unrecognizable. When in an elevated state of fear, bosses can become blind to the impact they are having on others around them.

Is it Me? Is it my Boss? Is it Us? Is it the Company?

These are some of the early questions people ask when they find themselves in confusing or threatening power dynamics.

Is it me? Maybe yes.

When the answer is yes, it's usually because something unique within you has been triggered, or you are only seeing things through your own perspective without taking a broader view.

When it's a personal trigger, others aren't reacting to the same dynamics in the same way as you, or at all. There will be patterns in your past where you've had run-ins, conflict and similar reactions to the same type of relationship dynamic where others haven't. You will be using terms like "always" and "never" and will feel others just aren't getting how atrocious the person or situation is.

When you have a myopic view and are only seeing things from your perspective, you will tend to generalize things, become judgmental and close out other viewpoints, and will only be interested in colluding with those who share the same perspective as you. You may have very little to no doubt that your truth is THE truth. You may cling to the idea that you are a powerless victim and there is no choice in playing a different role within the dynamic.

Unfortunately, when it's you, you usually can't see it. It takes courage and vulnerability to open yourself up to a different perspective from an honest critic.

Is it them? Could be.

You know it's them when others around you are reacting to the same dynamics and having the same friction with the person. You also know it's them when it is clearly a breach of company ethics or the law.

Is it us? Yes.

We've all heard the expression "It takes two to tango". Whether it's communication style, work standards or personality type, we almost all have had bad chemistry with someone, somewhere along the line.

Often, that bad chemistry can come from the personal filters we have that affect how we see people and situations.

Those filters are embedded within us as they are formed over time by where we come from geographically, our ethnic and cultural backgrounds and our inherited family of origin beliefs, attitudes and perspectives. Many people, unless they have had specific training or self-development to explore these filters, are usually blind to them. This often results in them showing up in what we say and do, unknowingly to us, but glaringly to another who may be sensitive to them.

When these clashes occur it's not too hard to spot them from the outside. Some examples are;

- Introvert vs extrovert
- High standards clash with average to lower standards
- Communication style, i.e., ask vs tell
- Visionary vs. structured
- Creative vs. analytical
- Driven for results vs low-keyed determination
- Lack of awareness of personal filters that triggers feelings of insensitivity to others

If we can't see the contrast, usually others around us can.

Is it the Organization? Could be.

We're talking about the organizational DNA here, the actual structure, culture, processes and procedures within an organization that allow for inconsistencies. These can include:

- Top performers getting different and special treatment and being exempt from the same rules as everyone else,
- Unclear policies regarding how to handle incivility in the workplace,
- A company rewards system that glorifies money and power while the company values promote humility and service orientation,
- Performance metrics that incentivize financial results over respectful behavior and ethical conduct,
- Unclear or non-existent policy and procedures for resolving issues and conflict,
- Weak excuses from leadership for bad behavior,

- Enforced policies related to inappropriate employee conduct with people at lower levels, and immunity provided to those higher up in the organization, even when inappropriate conduct at the senior level is witnessed by many,
- Ambiguity about what there is a tolerance for in the organization,
- Lack of skill development courses and resources in order to address difficult situations.

How This Book Works

In the introduction and chapter 1 we lay the foundation for what is to come. We give you the context you'll need to understand and use the models we propose in the resolution process, where we illustrate *how* to navigate the storm.

Chapters 2, 3, 4 and 5 are stories that illustrate a variety of power dynamics often seen in the workplace. Each story represents a different degree of egregiousness and threat. At the end of each story we end on a note where the elephant is left sitting in the middle of the room and someone is left stuck in a seemingly complex or no-win situation.

Chapter 6 gives a full explanation of the L.E.A.D. model, which is the actual process for finding resolution, and the Cringe Factor self-diagnostic to determine how threatening the situation is for you.

Chapter 7 shows the L.E.A.D. model and the Cringe Factor diagnostic in action relative to each of the four stories in chapters 2, 3, 4 and 5, and we tell you how each of the four stories ended. We illustrate how the resolution process was used in each story, and how the elephant in the room was confronted.

Chapter 8 gives areas of self-mastery leaders can focus on to build their courage muscle and become more resilient.

Chapter 9 is for those who like things that get to the point quickly and easily. We give you all the important points in this book in pictures and graphics for you to refer to quickly, any time you need it.

And last, chapter 10 is a shameless plug for the additional resources we offer at The Integreship_{SM}Group to support leaders in navigating the tough stuff.

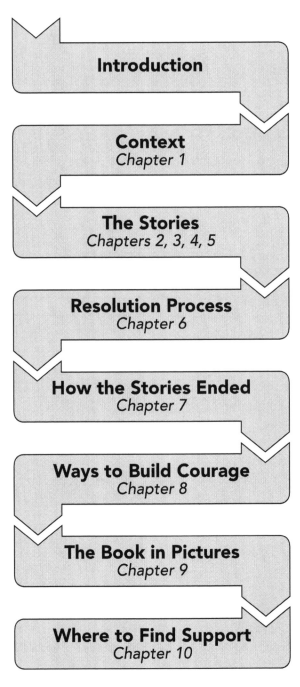

Chapter 2

Guilty before Proven Innocent

You don't know what you don't know

It was a routine meeting, just like many others in the past year, but Derrek, a senior engagement manager with a tech consulting firm, was feeling uptight. It seemed everyone in the room was uneasy too, because something was different with their boss Anna. She had an unfamiliar edge in her tone. Many in the room began discreetly glancing towards Derrek, the unofficial yet likely leadership successor to Anna.

Engaging with the New Boss – A Honeymoon Period

As their new boss, Anna had come into the company from a competitor a year before, and the team was excited to be working with her, given her reputation in the consulting business was outstanding. As a senior principal, Anna was very skilled at building bridges between the client, senior management and the engagement managers. She solicited others' ideas and collaborated in working through problems when needed. She advocated for the engagement managers when they needed it most, and the team felt secure knowing she always had their back. Though Anna could be tough at times, she was consistently fair, heard people out and treated them with respect — that was, until two months ago.

The Boss – Team Marriage Gets Tested

Derrek began noticing a shift in Anna's behavior shortly after a large contract had been landed with a new client, putting a temporary strain on the team. Overnight, it seemed that Anna had shifted from being inclusive and collaborative to unilateral in her decision-making. She began getting short-tempered and, at times, abruptly interrupted people in mid-sentence by talking over them in an irritated tone. Derrek also noticed Anna checking out in team meetings by answering emails and text messages, as if nothing in the meeting was important enough for her attention.

Derrek didn't want to admit it, but he was beginning to feel the team had been strategically courted and manipulated by Anna in the first months of her tenure, and now they were seeing the *real* Anna, more secure and a bit arrogant in her role after one year's successful performance. Derrek had worked more closely with Anna than anyone. She had made him her right-hand man as a senior engagement manager, and Derrek was also seeing the shift in her behavior now, more than anyone else on the team, because of their close working relationship. But the team member glances towards him in the meeting that morning told him everyone was seeing it now, and certainly feeling it, as Anna curtly delivered the news that the client wanted to move the current project deadline up by a month. Derrek and the rest of the team knew that Anna was asking for the impossible, given that the EM team had already been working evenings and weekends since they got the contract two months prior, and each EM was pushing their people to do the same. He knew someone had to say something to Anna about this tension, and he knew it needed to be him.

In that morning meeting, he explained to Anna that they had maxed out their people resources for this client, and given the imminent project deadlines, he asked her for her ideas on finding the resources to hit their project deadline date. Anna snapped back, "Derrek, this is why I made you senior engagement manager. I need YOU to be the creative thinker in situations like this — NOT ME!". The room went silent as Anna began packing up her laptop and left the room. The team sat there stunned for a minute, and then eyes began to look up, glancing towards Derrek. Derrek threw his hands up in the air and said, "I guess the honeymoon is over, folks, and we're now all married to the Dragon Lady!" There were a few nervous chuckles around the table.

The Boss is Guilty Before Proven Innocent

The climate remained the same for several weeks. The team dealt with it by engaging in sarcasm and dark humor at Anna's expense when she wasn't around. At lunch one day, with a couple of colleagues from another department, Derrek began inferring to them that Anna was a first class manipulator. He said she'd really pulled the wool over his eyes in those first months to get the team in her camp. He went on to talk about her rudeness and change in character over the past few months. One of Derrek's colleagues, Carla, asked if he thought it had anything to do with Anna's personal situation. Derrek gave her a puzzled look.

Carla said, "Don't you know, Derrek? My son is in Anna's son's class and he told me about what happened to Anna's father. He had a massive stroke about three months ago and he's been living at her house since his release from the hospital. Her father is recuperating slowly, but it's been really hard on their family." Derrek admitted that he had no idea that that had happened. Anna had never said a word about it. Derrek felt awful.

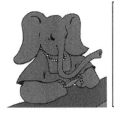

The elephant in the room:

Normally congenial co-worker or boss begins to demonstrate erratic or unacceptable behavior.

Turn to chapter 7 to see how Derrek took charge and how he confronted the elephant in the room.

Chapter 3

Your Job is to Make Me Look Good

Managing Perceptions Upwards

Sondra, a healthcare administrator and team lead on a policy overhaul project, walked out of the team meeting feeling flattened and tired. For weeks she had been trying to understand where things were breaking down within the team, but it all seemed like a jumbled mix of conversations and puzzling actions. On this day, however, it became crystal clear about where the problem was, and everything pointed towards Tom.

Nice Guy, No Accountability

Tom had come on the team late because he was finishing up another project which went past deadline. He was quickly brought up to date by Sondra and a couple of other team members. No one on the team had worked with Tom before as he had only been working for the healthcare network for a little less than a year. Everyone seemed to like Tom and got along well with him. He had great executive presence and people gravitated towards him as a natural leader. In addition, he was very creative and resourceful when it came to brainstorming sessions and thinking out of the box. Tom had a lot going for him except for one very important thing. He was relatively unaccountable to the team. He frequently missed scheduled meetings and didn't take time to read over the meeting notes the team kept. It was made quite clear by Jackie, the administrative director, that this project was to become each team member's priority, as their work was dovetailing into a much larger policy initiative for all six hospitals in their healthcare network.

Tom was clearly not making this project a priority. He'd drop in after a week or two of missed meetings and then would begin asking questions to be brought up to speed. After a couple of times doing this, Sondra pulled Tom aside and explained to him that bringing him up to speed each time he missed meetings pulled the team backwards and wasted precious time. With the deadline looming, Sondra explained they couldn't keep doing this. Tom nodded and agreed with her and said he'd try to do better, but he had a lot of competing priorities and their boss Jackie knew this when she asked him to be part of this team. It struck Sondra as a little odd that Tom felt he had a different level of responsibility than everyone else on the team, including Sondra, and didn't consider himself as a peer. They all had a desk full of competing priorities, but she let it go.

Wrong! Now Go Fix It.

Tom continued to helicopter in and out of the project after Sondra had talked to him. Much of the structure and framework for the project had been established by the team without his help, because Tom had only attended about one third of the meetings. When he did come in, he'd offer a constructive and useful critique of the work that had been done by the team. Because of Tom's strong presence and his self-assured way of interacting with team members, he began to position himself as an outside authority looking in on their work. It began to set up an unspoken and insidious dynamic where the team began to act as if they were reporting to Tom and awaiting his approval and buy-in before finalizing anything. On several occasions this meant going back to the drawing board and re-doing what had already been done, without Tom rolling up his sleeves and jumping in to do the work himself.

This dynamic continued and worsened. Tom never offered suggestions on what *should* be done, only criticism and thoughts on what didn't work. More than once, this resulted in making corrections to work that had been done more than once and increased the subtle team dynamic of winning Tom's approval even more.

Visibility and Recognition? Now You Have My Attention.

About four months into the project their boss Jackie sat in on one of their team meetings. Tom happened to be present at that meeting and had positioned himself next to her. Several times throughout the meeting Tom leaned over and whispered comments into Jackie's ear. Sondra began to feel unsettled as she was beginning to see Tom behave in an even more hierarchal manner with Jackie present, setting himself apart from the team in a very subtle, yet unmistakable way. Jackie acknowledged the team for their hard work and said that she was very impressed with the structure they'd built for their overhaul. Tom chimed in several times as if he'd been there right from the start and was a constant presence in building that structure, even though he'd attended only one third of the meetings and came in late after all the initial structure had been built.

After that meeting it was as if Tom took a renewed interest in the project and began dedicating more time to it. He still did not originate work himself or take on specific deliverables, but attended more meetings and continued offering his criticism. The team began to see through Tom's motives. It was apparent he wanted to be more involved once he learned Jackie had used their process as an example to other teams working on the larger policy initiative. He was blatantly managing how senior management was perceiving his role and contributions.

The team began pressuring Tom to take on deliverables between meetings. They also began to hold him accountable to correct the areas he was criticizing himself versus having team members run off to do his bidding for him. He'd say yes to taking on the deliverables, but consistently didn't produce and felt no need to apologize to the team for his delinquency.

How Dare You Speak Ungrateful People!

They were six weeks out from deadline when heated words began to get exchanged in the meetings between the team and Tom. Tom was outraged by the confrontations and truly didn't get why everyone was so upset. It became very apparent Tom held himself as an outsider who shouldn't be held to the same standards as the rest of the team. He said he felt attacked and didn't know where all this anger was coming from. And that's when he dropped the bomb that made the room go silent. He heatedly said that it was obvious why Jackie assigned him to this team. She wanted to ensure it stayed on track because she knew it was under weak leadership and that if it weren't for him, their work would have gone careening off the rails a long time ago. He went on to say that he wasn't about to trust the team to produce a final body of work with his name on it without strong direction from him.

Once she was able to recover from this astounding statement, Sondra asked Tom if Jackie had asked him specifically to take on this particular role with the team. Tom said she hadn't, but it was implied in her initial conversation with him and that it became obvious to him once he witnessed the team dynamics and lack of leadership that he had to step in with strong direction. Tom had clearly tipped his hand for all to see. He never did consider himself a member of the team and instead held himself in an elite role that he'd fabricated for himself to protect and promote himself as well as keep him from being accountable to the team with his own deliverables. Tempers continued to flare and the tension in the room could be cut with a knife when Ravi, a fellow team member, asked Tom what the team could expect from him until the project was completed, since he clearly saw himself in a different role than the rest of the team. Tom said he had another meeting he had to get to but would address that in their next meeting.

Two days later everyone began filtering into the room for their 9:00 AM meeting. The entire team was present, except for Tom. The team waited until 9:15 and still no Tom. Sondra called his office and got his voice-mail. Apparently he was at work that day, but chose not to come to the meeting. Sondra and the rest of the team were at their wits end with him and moving forward with him on the team would only create more tension. Sondra knew something had to be done and as team lead, felt it was her role to take the initiative.

> ### The elephant in the room:
> *Managing up to look good while disrespecting or dismissing others.*

Turn to chapter 7 to see how Sondra took charge and confronted the elephant in the room.

Chapter 4

The Emperor Who Sucked Up
And Thought Decency was for Show Only

Margot had been an executive assistant for 17 years. She loved what she did and knew her job well. She had worked for and alongside a number of senior executives over the years, most of them wonderful, a few of them difficult. With all that experience behind her, nothing had prepared her to work with someone like Jason.

Enter the Emperor

Margot's previous boss, Jack, had retired the year before and Jason was brought in from outside the company to replace him as marketing VP. At first, Margot was excited at the prospect of working with an executive brought in from the outside. She looked forward to helping Jason integrate into the organizational culture and become successful with his colleagues and team. It didn't take long for Margot to realize that Jason was not open to partnering with her because he clearly viewed executive assistants as lower status employees, a necessary headcount expense to manage leadership appointment scheduling and to attend to concierge-type requests.

From Executive Assistant to Personal Assistant

It began on his third day on the job when Jason handed Margot a piece of paper at 2:00 and said, "Here's the address of my son's school. You need to be there by 3:00 PM sharp when he's done with school, and then take him home. My wife will take it from there. If my wife isn't home

yet, just stay with him for a few minutes until she gets there." Margot was stunned. In all the years she had been an Executive Assistant, no one she worked for had just assumed she'd do personal errands and especially in such a demanding tone. She decided right then to say something to Jason so this didn't set a precedent in their working relationship. She explained to him that in her 17 years working for senior leadership in the organization, it wasn't the norm to ask EAs to run personal errands, though she'd be happy to help him out this time. She asked if he could make different arrangements for his personal matters in the future. Jason continued to multi-task by staring and typing into his phone, and then without looking up from his device, replied: "So tell me, is this in the company policy book anywhere?" Margot said she didn't know. Jason shot a quick glance up from his screen and said in an arrogant tone: "Then I suggest you find out. And if it isn't there, then I could care less about what is customary in this company." Margot began to respectfully respond when Jason's cellphone rang; he answered it in the middle of her first sentence and dived into his telephone conversation as if Margot wasn't even in the room. Margot turned and walked out with a sick feeling in her stomach.

Enter the Suck-Up

Similar treatment continued for several weeks. Margot continued to push back, but there was no progress in establishing any kind of a productive working relationship with Jason, given the absence of respect. Margot knew she couldn't last long with things this way.

The watershed moment came two months later when Jason called and told her to bring his laptop down to the boardroom. Margot entered the room while all the senior executives were on a short break from the meeting and milling around the room, including Ken, the CEO. Ken always had a kind word for Margot and frequently asked about her dog Ralph when he saw her, as they were both dog lovers. When Margot set down Jason's laptop on the conference room table, he graciously thanked her within earshot of the other executives in the room. Margot was stunned because this was literally the first time he'd ever thanked her. As Margot was leaving, Ken was getting some coffee and talking to Laura, the president of the company and Jason's boss. Ken said hello to Margot and asked her how Ralph was doing. Margot said old Ralph was doing great and asked how Ken's dogs were. At that exact moment, Jason walked up and inserted himself into the conversation by saying

in a jovial tone, "I was asking Margot about Ralph the other day too. There seem to be several of us who are dog nuts around here. Ralph couldn't be luckier. If she takes care of him half as well as she takes care of all she does for me, he's the luckiest dog in the world!"

Margot was clearly taken back by Jason's sudden chumminess, and Laura quickly picked up on it because she and Margot had a good relationship and had worked closely for many years. Laura immediately stepped in and changed the subject. Margot said her goodbyes and left the room. When Margot returned to her office, she took a moment to collect herself and reflect upon what she had just experienced. She knew Jason was one to manage perceptions to those equal or above him, but she never thought he'd make up untrue stories to politically ingratiate himself with senior leadership.

Margot decided it was time to act. All of the previous attempts she'd made to push back to her boss were ignored, and worse, were turned back on her with Jason's sarcasm and dismissive comments.

The elephant in the room:

Abusing title and organizational role — unrealistic and inappropriate demands of others

Turn to chapter 7 to see how Margot took charge and confronted the elephant in the room.

Chapter 5

The Lonely Road of Integrity
Doing Right When There is No One to Do it but Yourself

The Land of Opportunity – Working Your Way Up

Raised in India and having immigrated to the U.S. at 16 years old, Binder worked hard to learn English and to finish school. He attended a community college in New Jersey and was offered a machinist position at a nearby manufacturer after receiving his 2-year Associate's degree.

A quick learner, Binder was soon promoted to supervisor. That's when things began to change for him. He wasn't on the job long when he noticed some work slowdowns in the three manufacturing lines he was responsible for. When asked, line workers would tell Binder there were problems with the machines. They said they were waiting for parts, along with a few other excuses that didn't ring true to Binder. He became suspicious there was more to the line slowdowns than he was being told and spent several evenings pouring over inventory records. The records revealed inconsistencies in materials and supplies and strongly suggested something was amiss.

When You See Something, Say Something

Binder met weekly with his employees. During one group meeting shortly after finding the inventory inconsistencies, he expressed concern that the inventory control records were not matching the actual inventory. He asked if anyone could explain what might be happening. Blank looks and silence followed. Two days later a threatening message was sent to Binder when he saw his car had been deliberately scratched from the front to the back. As he drove home he knew he had to do something in spite of the threat.

The next morning Binder went to his manager Tony to share what he had discovered in the inventory records, and to raise concerns over the vandalism to his car in the work parking lot. Tony dismissed Binder's concerns by saying, "If there is theft happening, it happens in every company. The bean counters at corporate make adjustments for this. It's really not worth making accusations and disrupting the entire production force. Besides, there are a few tough guys out there, and provoking them may go beyond keying our cars."

Feeling unsupported and discounted by his manager, Binder decided he could not ignore this ethically, even if his boss Tony didn't feel it was necessary to confront the situation. He decided to talk to Kara, the director of human resources. He scheduled a meeting with her and shared the same information. To his dismay, Kara also dismissed Binder's concerns and told him he couldn't prove anything with the inventory or the car. She minimized his concerns and said that making accusations without proof could make trouble for everyone. Kara advised Binder to tone down his concerns about theft and focus more on increasing production yield and maintaining a good safety track record. Clearly both Tony and Kara were afraid of the line workers and afraid of what they might do if the situation got escalated.

A week later, Tony and Kara called Binder into a meeting and suggested he work with an external executive coach to improve his management style and work on his leadership skills. Binder was stunned that his attempt to be ethical and upright had now been turned back on him, implying that he was the one with the problem.

Within a week, Binder and the coach met for the first time. His new coach, Kathrine, informed him that she was told he was going to be put on a performance plan and moved out of the company if he didn't stop intimidating the employees he supervised, and that it was required that he turn around his management style. She went on to say that everything they talked about would be strictly confidential and that while she was hired by his company, she was also here to fully support Binder in whatever way he needed. She then asked him about his side of what had transpired and why he thought his job was on the line.

Taking a Risk – Doing the Right Thing

Binder told Katherine that no one above him would listen to his concerns about the potential theft or investigate further. He said he felt frustrated because he had strong evidence in the inventory control records to suggest there was indeed theft happening in their plant. He added that his car had been vandalized two days after he met with the line workers. He believed he had exhausted all of his options to find a resolution. Katherine quickly picked up on the essence of Binder's hopelessness and asked him why he cared so much when no one else did. Binder said his father had chosen the name "Binder" for him which meant brave leader in Hindi. His father instilled in him that he was born into life to act with courage and do the right thing. Binder shared with his coach that his father died two years after his family moved to the U.S., and that Binder had vowed to make his father proud by living up to the noble name he had been given.

> ### *The elephant in the room:*
> *Unethical, illegal, or out-of-policy conduct — visible to many and unaddressed.*

Turn to chapter 7 to see how Binder took charge and confronted the elephant in the room.

Chapter 6

Navigating the Storm

The storm is what we like to call a Cringe Moment. Those moments of truth where something has been said or done by someone else and it cannot go ignored and must be faced. There may be months, or even years, of egregious situations that lead up to a Cringe Moment, but there is almost always a watershed point where the final straw breaks the camel's back. Taking charge of a Cringe Moment requires having the right tools to navigate the storm. You'll want tools to help you weigh out risks, options and rewards in order to be confident that whatever risk you take or don't take is right for you given all the circumstances.

Trusting yourself to resolve a Cringe Moment means knowing your decision(s) has been well thought out, with all considerations taken and a plan to move forward with calculated actions. In this chapter we will give you the navigation tools in our L.E.A.D. model which will guide you with personalized coordinates for getting through a Cringe Moment storm with your integrity intact.

L.E.A.D. Yourself to Resolution

The L.E.A.D. model utilizes proven steps and techniques used by professional coaches to coach their clients to resolution. It is designed to use by yourself or with someone else if you are helping them get through a difficult situation. Let's begin with the meaning of the acronym.

In this section you will discover how to get down to what is really happening and how much of a threat the situation poses. You will also learn how to identify what values are at play, how they are being compromised and how to get realigned with them. And last, you'll be given a process for identifying the best possible action to take for integrity-based resolution.

Let's begin!

Learn the Story

Have you ever gotten greater clarity or had an "aha moment" while relating a story to someone else? Talking things out with a good listener allows powerful and sometimes unconscious reactions, beliefs, attitudes and perceptions to emerge. It provides an opportunity to reexamine and reframe how you are seeing or experiencing something and allows for a fresh perspective.

Take the time to recount what is happening or has happened either by writing the story down or talking it out with someone you consider to be a good listener and a neutral VOR (voice of reason). This is especially helpful if there has been a series of events over time which has led up to a Cringe Moment. It allows you to string all the pieces and moving parts together as well as having the cathartic experience of downloading and expressing the emotions you may be feeling.

Along the way you may learn new things about yourself and your role, or see what is happening differently. The goal is to allow the tide of emotions and reactions to go out while recounting the story. Once the emotion goes out, it uncovers what lies below the upset, i.e. beliefs, attitudes, perceptions and the facts. This will help you establish a framework of what is really going on while reducing personal distortions. Which leads us to the next thing we need to learn before we get into sorting out options, risks and rewards.

Know Thy Cringe Factor Level

Your Cringe Factor Level is a self-determined rating of four factors that indicate your personal threat level from a Cringe Moment.

You may be experiencing any of the following when in a Cringe Moment:

- Feeling of dread
- Wanting to avoid confrontation
- Feeling stuck without choices
- Instant odd feeling about what has just been said or done
- Fearful that you don't have the skills or language to address it
- Feeling alone
- Obsessing about it
- Thinking it will only get worse if you try to change it
- Feeling powerless
- Losing sleep over it
- Overwhelmed and confused
- Concerned or panicked about how the other person will react

Everyone processes Cringe Moments differently. What one person feels exceedingly threatened by, another person may feel only irritation. The causes that influence what gets triggered within us when encountering a Cringe Moment are as diverse and unique as every person is. These moments of truth manifest in a multitude of feelings from discomfort to paralyzed. The feelings we have and the degree to which we feel them are idiosyncratic. It is important to identify what you are feeling, because it impacts your ability to reason.

Reason and logic happen in the frontal and prefrontal cortex of the human brain. It is the part of the brain that houses executive functions, where more complex reasoning occurs. Without the executive function we would not have the ability to make decisions, plan and problem solve. With it, we are able to have:

- Discernment
- Judgment
- Impulse control
- Mental flexibility
- Insight and self-knowledge
- Empathy
- Integrity

All very important aspects to navigating Cringe Moments; however, as an individual's perceived threat level goes higher, their ability to tap into the executive function of their brain lowers, because the human brain is hardwired to deprioritize that part

> *When presented with a threat, the human brain is biologically hardwired to deprioritize the part of the brain that supports sound reasoning and shifts to prioritize the part of the brain that supports survival.*

of the brain when faced with a threat and instead prioritizes the part of the brain concerned only with survival. Essentially, the bigger the threat, the lower the executive brain function.

It was great when humans were threatened by saber-toothed tigers and woolly mammoths, however, beneath the frontal lobes is a part of the brain that is dedicated just to survival. That part of the brain doesn't know or care about the difference between your boss who just dressed you down in a meeting and a prehistoric bird swooping in to carry you away from the meeting room table in its talons. There is a cascade of biological functions that kick in to ensure we are maximized energetically to fight or flee when faced with a threat. Part of that energy efficiency system is to shut down the executive function of the brain. Great for squaring off with a woolly mammoth, not so great when going toe-to-toe with your boss.

Using the Cringe Factor self-diagnostic tool, you can get a gauge on how much you can rely on the part of your brain that allocates executive functions to assist you in sound reasoning when navigating a Cringe Moment. Here's how to use the Cringe Factor tool.

Step 1: Feeling Assessment

Determine what you are feeling about the situation. Feelings are the language of the deepest parts of our character. Getting in touch with exactly what feelings you are associating with your situation will connect you with that part of yourself that also holds your conscience, courage and integrity.

Cringe Factor 1: Bothered

You may be annoyed or frustrated by what someone has said or done. It has you a little rattled and feelings are relatively low level without interfering in anything else in your life. Feeling little to no fear.

Cringe Factor 2: Worried

Upset and distracted, you are feeling a mild level of fear and uncertainty about what may happen or potential consequences that could come. You are still able to separate your feelings about the person/situation from other parts of your life.

Cringe Factor 3: Anguished

You are feeling troubled and anxious and are beginning to suffer because of the situation. The feelings you have for the situation are bleeding over and stealing positive feelings from other parts of your life.

Cringe Factor 4: Threatened

You are feeling trapped, exposed and vulnerable. Danger feels imminent. Feelings about the person/situation have dominated and crowded out feelings for anything else.

Cringe Factor Level Feelings

4 — Threatened, panicked, afraid, unsafe, intimidated, exposed, vulnerable, jeopardized, unprotected, overwhelmed, at risk, attacked, bullied, coerced, pressured, denounced

3 — Anguished, despair, miserable, strained, overcome, stewing, agonizing, suffering, dejected, oppressed, pained, tormented, crushed, troubled, humiliation, mistreated, exploited, offended

2 — Worried, upset, distressed, bad vibes, flustered, apprehensive, on edge, suspicious, upset, stunned, mistrustful, troubled, uncertain, tense, uneasy, alarmed, shaken, judged

1 — Bothered, discouraged, marginalized, distracted, concerned, agitated, provoked, unbalanced, irked, frustrated, annoyed, bugged, undermined, rattled, insulted, disappointed, confused, misled

 ## Step 2: Thinking Assessment

Gauge how much bandwidth the situation is taking up in your thinking. How often you think about the situation is a distinct indicator as to which part of your brain is engaged and how much executive function is available to you for sound reasoning.

Cringe Factor 1: Momentary Thinking

You think about the situation for just a moment perhaps a couple of times a day. It usually doesn't pop up on your radar until you are reminded in some way and then only a few seconds of brain space is used on it.

Cringe Factor 2: Frequent Thinking

The space between when you think about the situation and when you don't becomes shorter. You are thinking about it several times a day. At times when you are reminded by something, and even when you aren't, it pops up in your awareness without warning or reason.

Cringe Factor 3: Constant Thinking

Thinking about the situation is happening without pause and is regular and persistent. You are able to focus on other things; however, thoughts of the situation interfere with your concentration and focus without letting up. There is no pushing it aside.

Cringe Factor 4: Dominant Thinking

The situation becomes the predominant thought. You become completely preoccupied with thinking about it. It pushes out almost all other thoughts. It is with you morning, noon and night and even the simplest routine tasks require extra concentration.

 ## Step 3: Risk Assessment

In this step you will assess the level of risk associated with confronting the person(s) and/or the situation.

Cringe Factor 1: Low

Historically, you have a good working relationship and open dialog is customary. You have been able to have sensitive dialogs that were civil and respectful. You have very little reason to believe it would be any different if you were to confront the current situation. You are interacting with a reasonable person who you feel is mature enough to introspectively examine their role and own their mistake/behavior/role/oversight, if needed. You are fairly confident the confrontation won't put your job, career, reputation or relationship at risk.

Cringe Factor 2: Moderate

You may have a history of witnessing unpredictable reactions or feel the confrontation could touch a nerve or trigger a negative reaction in the person. Normally, the person is reasonable, but you have observed random negative reactions that were either unwarranted, confusing or over-reactions with yourself or others. There is a slight chance that confrontation could affect your job, career, reputation and relationship with the person being confronted and/or possibly others.

Cringe Factor 3: Elevated

Confronting the situation means laying out specific behaviors/actions that you are relatively certain will spark a negative reaction in the person. You are expecting defensiveness and anger when naming the elephant, and perhaps veiled threats. There is a significant risk that a confrontation could impact your job, career, reputation and relationship in negative ways.

Cringe Factor 4: High

You have witnessed a consistent pattern of angry outbursts, irrational reactions or retaliatory behavior from the person. The situation to be confronted can also be so egregious (i.e., illegal or unethical behavior) that there is certain to be a red-alert defensive position from the person, who may go on the offense to discredit you or your allegations. The person has the power and the likelihood of severely threatening your job, career, reputation and relationship with others.

 ## *Step 4: Options Assessment*

Usually, as the threat level increases, your options for resolving the situation decrease, but that isn't always the case. This step requires an examination of those options from the obvious to the farfetched. In using this section of the Cringe Factor tool, you may find you come upon some options you hadn't considered previously. Bonus! It will also be an important component in evaluating the overall landscape of the threat itself and designing the actions you want to take. It is important to step outside of seeing only what is comfortable or slightly uncomfortable for you and to list options that would be uncomfortable to highly uncomfortable. Here's how to rate your options;

Cringe Factor 1: Multiple

You can see many options available to you but are not certain which will be the most effective. Some may seem less plausible than others initially; however, it is important to list them as options at this stage. You will usually be able to see at least five options to rate it multiple. Remember, from obvious to farfetched get listed.

Cringe Factor 2: Narrowing

You are only able to see three or four options available to resolve the situation for you and it could be that the situation is escalating or can escalate further, narrowing your options even more.

Cringe Factor 3: Limited

You are down to an either/or situation. The options are fairly clear-cut and obvious. You're usually looking at only two options in this category and neither one is comfortable or without risk.

Cringe Factor 4: Singular

There is only one option visible and it has definite risk associated with it.

Step 5: Determine Your Level

Now that you've rated all four of the Cringe Factors, use the Cringe Factor level number associated with your choices (example: 2 for Worried, 2 for Frequent, 3 for Elevated, 2 for Narrowing). Add up the total of the numbers associated with each Cringe Factor you've chosen. For example, the total on the Cringe Factor choices below would be 9. Then divide that number by 4 to get your final Cringe Factor level.

Cringe Factor		Feeling	Thinking	Risk to Comfort	Options
	1	Bothered	Momentary	Lower	Multiple
	2	(Worried)	(Frequent)	Moderate	(Narrowing)
	3	Anguished	Constant	(Elevated)	Limited
	4	Threatened	Dominant	High	Singular

2 (Worried) +
2 (Frequent) +
3 (Elevated) +
2 (Narrowing) =
___
9

9 ÷ 4 = 2.25
Cringe Factor Level: 2

Now What?

If you have a Cringe Factor level 3 or 4, we strongly recommend getting a Voice of Reason (VOR) involved as there is a high likelihood you are operating with reduced executive brain function and may miss crucial elements in the process of navigating the steps that will lead you to resolution.

A Voice of Reason is extremely helpful and recommended at any Cringe Factor level; however, executive brain functions are usually operating at enough capacity to self-navigate at Cringe Factor level 1 or 2. We are not suggesting that you become unreasonable at Cringe Factor 3 and 4 by suggesting a voice of reason instead it's to see broader and farther through the perspective of someone else who is not threatened by the situation since your perceptions narrow due to the increased threat and reduced executive brain function.

If you elect to engage a VOR, *who you* choose is very important. Here are some characteristics to consider when choosing:

- Emotionally mature
- Seasoned in successfully navigating difficult situations with others themselves
- Impartial and objective
- Honest and supportive
- Drama-free type of person
- Firm, articulate and compassionate
- Resourceful

Some VOR sources to consider would be a former boss, a friend who you know can be an honest critic, a person you have formally or informally considered a mentor and of course a coach.

EXPLORE
VALUES

Explore the Values in Jeopardy

No matter our background, culture, social status, gender or age, we all share five distinct values that are directly connected to our moral compass and sense of right and wrong.

They are:

- Fairness
- Honesty
- Compassion
- Respect
- Responsibility[4]

Recognizing which values are most in jeopardy can be a bit tricky though. You'll likely discover most, or all of them, are at play in any given situation. We want to get it narrowed down to the one, or in some instances two, that are most in jeopardy. In order to do that you will need a good understanding of what is happening when each value is protected and when they are in jeopardy.

Fairness	
When fairness is upheld you will experience:	**When fairness is in jeopardy you will experience:**
Civility	Marginalization
Decency	Lack of consistency
Tolerance	Rudeness
Honor	Injustice
Justice	Partiality
Reasonable	Favoritism
Give-and-take	Biased
Open mindedness	Unilateral decisions

---

4   Table 1: "Proposed Shared Values" [p. 47] from MORAL COURAGE by RUSHWORTH M. KIDDER. Copyright (c) 2005 by Rushworth M. Kidder. Reprinted by permission of HarperCollins Publishers.

Honesty

When honesty is upheld you will experience:	When honesty is in jeopardy you will experience:
Candor	Lying
Frankness	Dishonesty
Genuine	Embellishment
Loyalty	Disloyalty
Morality	Immorality
Sincerity	Cheating
Virtue	Fraudulent behavior
Conscientiousness	Deception
Authenticity	
Principled	

Compassion

When compassion is upheld you will experience:	When compassion is in jeopardy you will experience:
Benevolence	Animosity
Empathy	Cruelty
Humaneness	Ill Will
Kindness	Uninterested
Sympathy	Meanness
Responsiveness	Mercilessness
Concern	Harshness
	Indifference
	Apathy
	Coldness

Respect	
When respect is upheld you will experience:	*When respect is in jeopardy you will experience:*
Appreciation Considerate behavior Honoring of dignity Regards wishes Recognition Courteousness Acknowledgement	Excessive criticism Disdain Disregard Disrespect Ignore Neglectfulness Disfavor Thoughtlessness

Responsibility	
When responsibility is upheld you will experience:	*When responsibility is in jeopardy you will experience:*
Accountability Commitment Answerable Prioritized Engagement Obligation Duty-bound	Blamelessness Irresponsibility Unreliable Untrustworthy Self-serving Self-exempted Immunity

ALIGN
VALUES TO OPTIONS

Align the Value in Jeopardy to Your Options

In this step you will take what is happening outside and turn it inwards. In doing this you will protect the value in jeopardy and restore your integrity. As we said earlier in this book, your integrity is intact when what you say and do aligns with your values.

In the previous step you identified which value is in jeopardy, which was most likely based on what the other person is doing and saying. For example, you may have chosen responsibility because your boss has asked you and your team to direct your focus and efforts on something that is obviously self-serving so she can manage optics to senior management. An outside influence (your boss) is putting the universal value of responsibility in jeopardy because she is acting irresponsibly in her own interest and asking you and your team to move off your team's target, which serves the mission and goals of the organization, and in to serving her personal objective.

When moving back into alignment with the value in jeopardy there is one cardinal rule to remember;

The only shift you can truly affect is a shift within yourself.

Shifting the value in jeopardy from outside to inside means that you take that value and use it as a decision-making filter for yourself when reviewing options. When faced with having to make a Cringe Moment decision we begin by taking the value at play and running it through the three most obvious choices:

1. Stay in your role/company and self-manage your reactions and emotions.
2. Address the person and/or situation directly.
3. Begin preparing an exit strategy.

Based on the value in jeopardy you chose, answer the following:

Which of these three options align me most with:

- Being **fair** to myself or others?
- Being **honest** with myself and others?
- Being **compassionate** towards myself and others?
- Being **respectful** towards myself and others?
- Being **responsible** to myself and others?

And what needs to be done by you to put it in place?

Again, working with a VOR in this step can be extremely beneficial. We also suggest that you write out your answers so you can reflect on them.

Putting Values in Action

You should now have a good idea of what your best option is and why. Now it's time to build a plan that will take you through preparation all the way to capturing what you've learned in the debrief. In the deployment stage of the model you will outline four key factors for readiness and action.

1. Prepare
2. Rehearse
3. Execute
4. Debrief

Prepare

List all you will need to prepare for whatever option you've chosen. If it's to stay and self manage, list how you'll prepare yourself to remain in neutral state or how you'll stay outside the toxic politics, for example. If you've chosen to address the person or situation, what will you need to enter into the meeting or confrontation? If putting an exit strategy in place is your choice, list what needs to be done before you can exit, such as updating your resume, getting additional training or certifications, or expanding your network.

Rehearse

One of the primary factors that stop or paralyze people from resolving Cringe Moments is fearing that they don't have the communication skills or language to address it. Rehearsing and scripting what you want to say will get you past that anxiety. You can write out your script, record it or work with a VOR to nail down what you want to say and how you want to say it. Rehearsing should give you a huge boost in feeling confident. Again, rehearsing works in all three options. Regardless of which one, scripting applies. If you are going to stay and self-manage, scripting is great to circumvent triggering situations or calmly respond to expected bad behavior. It goes without saying what the benefits of rehearsing are for addressing or confronting the situation. And if you choose to plan an exit strategy, what you will say in networking situations or to prospective employers is much more effective with a solid script you feel authentic using.

Execute

This is the step where you *pull the trigger*. This is where you set the meeting to say what needs to be said, or send the resumes out and/or interview for the job, or choose to opt out of a discussion, project or career move because you are self-managing. It's where preparation and action intersect.

Debrief

After you have made your choice, prepared, and set things in motion, there is always something to be learned or discovered on the back end of everything. Writing it all out and searching for the learning while writing is helpful, as is debriefing with a VOR.

Why Aligning and Acting on Values Is Important

In her book, *Giving Voice to Values: How to Speak Your Mind When You Know What's Right,* Dr. Mary Gentile clarifies it this way, "It is important because the fundamental stance we are taking in the Giving Voice to Values approach to values-driven action is one of alignment, of moving with our highest aspirations and our deepest sense of who we wish to be, rather than a stance of coercion and stern judgment, or of moving against our inclinations. Although self-discipline is certainly required to voice and act on our values, the emphasis here is on finding the part of ourselves that already wants to do this, and then empowering, enabling, training, and strengthening that self."[5]

---

5   Gentile, Mary C. Giving Voice to Values: How to Speak Your Mind When You Know What's Right. Yale University Press.

Before You Read Further, a Word About Comfort

If you are reading this book to find a comfortable way to move through a Cringe Moment that is without risk, you won't find it. Navigating Cringe Moments with integrity is hardly ever comfortable or tidy. There's no way to predict what will happen in any given situation, but we can help you minimize the risk and give you more confidence. In chapter 8 we'll also give you some ways to build resiliency and courage.

The L.E.A.D. Model in Action

Now that we've introduced you to the L.E.A.D. model to navigate a Cringe Moment to resolution, we'll move on to the outcome of the four stories in chapters 2 through 5. Each story reflected a Cringe Factor at each of the four levels. These stories are an amalgamation of common themes from stories we've heard or witnessed over the years. Read through these story outcomes and see how the main characters find resolution in each one.

Chapter 7

How the Stories Ended

Story 1
Guilty before Proven Innocent
You don't know what you don't know

> **The elephant in the room:**
>
> *Normally congenial co-worker or boss begins to demonstrate erratic or unacceptable behavior.*

LEARN
THE STORY
THE CRINGE FACTOR LEVEL

Derrek felt discouraged and frustrated. He really only thought about the situation with Anna when he was with her and her behavior was dismissive or short. He had had a good relationship with Anna before her behavior change, so his risk in talking to her about it was low too. He had several options in how he could approach Anna and the situation.

		Feeling	Thinking	Risk to Comfort	Options
Cringe Factor	**1**	Bothered	Momentary	Lower	Multiple
	2	Worried	Frequent	Moderate	Narrowing
	3	Anguished	Constant	Elevated	Limited
	4	Threatened	Dominant	High	Singular

$$1 + 1 + 1 + 1 = 4$$
$4 \div 4 = 1.0$ Cringe Factor

EXPLORE
VALUES

Once Derrek learned of Anna's personal struggles he shifted the value at play from *Respect to Compassion*. And it was HIS compassion that was at play.

What Derrek chose and why:

Honesty	Fairness	Respect	Compassion	Responsibility

Compassion *"Because I never considered that Anna's unexplainable behavior change could have had something to do with a personal issue at home. I just thought about my own feelings and reactions."*

In asking Derrek:

Which of these three options align you most with being **compassionate** toward yourself or others? And what needs to be done to put it in place?

He answered:

☒ **Stay and self manage**	☐ **Address the person directly**	☐ **Put exit strategy in place**
Compassion		
Now that I know this has to do with a personal issue I need to keep reminding myself of that when I get upset or angry over Anna's behavior or tone.		
I am going to cut her some slack and maybe even try to help her out more than I have been.		

DEPLOY
VALUES BASED ACTION

Prepare:	By going into meetings and interactions with Anna with a compassionate mindset.
Rehearse:	By practicing some different ways I can respond when she's being short or rude that won't make matters worse.
Execute:	By demonstrating compassion and understanding in the moment.
Debrief:	By talking through any tension caused by Anna in a productive way with an outsider versus gossiping and griping with others on the team.

HOW THE STORY ENDED
Derrek took charge of the elephant

Ten days after Derrek found out Anna was struggling with personal problems, Anna pulled the EM team together in a meeting and said she needed to apologize for her recent change in behavior. She went on to explain that her father had suffered a stroke that was life-altering, and that he was now living with her and her family. His doctors had said they needed a few months before they could determine the extent of the permanent damage he would have. Just after the stroke, he had lost control of his entire left side and his complete ability to speak. He couldn't walk or feed himself. The doctors said because her father was in good enough health prior to the stroke, they had hope for a fair amount of recovery, but they could not say to what extent. Anna shared that her father had been making good progress in rehabilitation and was regaining speech and movement. It seemed to be a slow recovery though the doctors were hopeful for considerable recovery in the next six months.

Anna went on to tell the team she may have made a mistake by not sharing this with the team earlier. Anna admitted that it wasn't fair how she had been treating people and that her ability to self manage her emotions at work had been lacking due to the suddenness and severity of the crisis on the home front. She apologized to the team and acknowledged them for their patience and understanding.

Derrek cleared his throat and said, "I'm so sorry for what you've been through, Anna. I think I can speak for everyone when I say we are here to help you and pitch in on whatever is needed to get the job done. You are the leader of our team, but we are a team and that means we can support you too."

Story 2
Your Job is to Make Me Look Good
Managing Perceptions

> **The elephant in the room:**
>
> *Managing up to look good while disrespecting or dismissing others.*

LEARN
THE STORY
THE CRINGE FACTOR LEVEL

Since Tom was a peer, Sondra felt the situation was a moderate threat. She was flustered by Tom's behavior and lack of accountability and stunned by his admission of how he saw his role on the team. She felt a low risk to confronting Tom and talked to him twice, but eventually felt she had only one option as Tom had caused a lot of animosity towards himself with the other

	Feeling	Thinking	Risk to Comfort	Options
1	(Bothered)	Momentary	(Lower)	Multiple
2	Worried	(Frequent)	Moderate	Narrowing
3	Anguished	Constant	Elevated	Limited
4	Threatened	Dominant	High	(Singular)

Cringe Factor

1 + 2 + 1 + 4 = 8

8 ÷ 4 = 2.0 Cringe Factor

team members, and that was to go to Tom's boss who had as-signed him to the team.

Sondra felt the value at play was Responsibility since Tom was not acting as a responsible member of the team. And even though they were peers, Sondra felt it was her responsibility as team lead on the project to confront the elephant (being the situation). While Respect and Fairness were certainly at play in this story, Responsibility was the most predominant value at play in Sondra's opinion.

What Sondra chose and why:

Honesty	Fairness	Respect	Compassion	Responsibility

Responsibility "Tom has taken no responsibility towards the team or the mission of the team. Instead he is only concerned with promoting his own agenda and making himself look good. As the lead on this team, I have a responsibility to ensure everyone is pulling their weight, which Tom is clearly not doing."

ALIGN
VALUES TO OPTIONS

In asking Sondra:

Which of these three options align you most with being **responsible** toward yourself or others? And what needs to be done to put it in place?

She answered:

☐ Stay and self manage	☒ **Address the person directly**	☐ Put exit strategy in place
	My attempts to talk to Tom have not changed anything and other team members confronting him has not worked either. I need to speak with Jackie to let her know that Tom has not held up his responsibility as a team member *I also need to let her know that keeping him on the team will disrupt workflow due to his lack of accountability and the tension that now exists with other members of the team.*	

DEPLOY
VALUES BASED ACTION

☑ **Prepare:** Pull meeting attendance records together and create a chart showing what team members have originated work to contribute to the project to present to Jackie.

☑ **Rehearse:** Write out bullet points of what I want to say to Jackie.

☑ **Execute:** Have the meeting with Jackie.

☑ **Debrief:** Connect with the team once Jackie has made her decision on what to do and debrief with them.

HOW THE STORY ENDED
How Sondra took charge of the elephant

Sondra's meeting with Jackie went well. She explained that she and other team members had tried to talk to Tom to no avail. Jackie was surprised to hear about Tom's lack of accountability and hands-on participation in the project. She said that she would talk to him that afternoon and inform him he was being removed from the team. She assured Sondra she would address each point she'd brought to her about Tom's behavior with him, and told Sondra to let her know if there was any hostility or disruption towards Sondra or any of the team members from Tom after she met with him.

The team went on to make their deadline and won an internal award later that year for the ingenuity they used to structure their policy revamp. It wound up becoming a standard to be used for future policy projects. Sondra was promoted to work for Jackie the following year as assistant administrative director.

Story 3

The Emperor Who Sucked Up
And Thought Decency was for Show Only

The elephant in the room:

Abusing title and organizational role — unrealistic and inappropriate demands of others

LEARN
THE STORY
THE CRINGE FACTOR LEVEL

Margot felt mistreated and humiliated by Jason's treatment of her. She realized in his moment of decency towards her, in front of his boss Laura and the CEO Ken, it clearly showed he knew right from wrong and respectful from disrespectful. She found herself dreading the next day each night and it was constantly on her mind. She had already confronted Jason a couple of times and all it resulted in was a higher level of verbal abuse from him. She felt she only had a couple of options left to resolve the problem.

		Feeling	Thinking	Risk to Comfort	Options
	1	Bothered	Momentary	Lower	Multiple
	2	Worried	Frequent	Moderate	Narrowing
	3	(Anguished)	(Constant)	Elevated	(Limited)
	4	Threatened	Dominant	(High)	Singular

Cringe Factor

$$3 + 3 + 4 + 3 = 13$$

13 ÷ 4 = 3.25 Cringe Factor

EXPLORE
VALUES

Margot felt two values were equally at play in this situation, and both weighed equally for her. She chose *Fairness* because Jason was unfair in what he asked of Margot and used intimidation to get it. He was unfair to her because he did not *Respect* her and saw her as less than himself because of her position as an executive assistant. Margot also realized she was being unfair to herself by allowing Jason to continue treating her as he had and she was losing her self-respect because of it.

What Margot chose and why:

Honesty	(Fairness)	(Respect)	Compassion	Responsibility

Fairness *"Jason has made unfair demands of me and makes it very clear that I am beneath him and unfairly intimidates me to get what he wants."*

Respect *"Jason has made it clear he has very little respect for me. He also masquerades, using fake respect to those above him by pretending to be a respectful and collegial boss with me."*

In asking Margot:

Which of these three options align you most with **fairness** and **respect** for yourself or others? And what needs to be done to put it in place?

She answered:

☐ Stay and self manage	☒ Address the person directly	☐ Put exit strategy in place
	Fairness *I need to be fair to myself and tell Laura about Jason's disrespectful behavior towards me.* **Respect** *I will reclaim my self respect by no longer allowing Jason to ignore my requests and concerns by getting a third party involved.*	

DEPLOY
VALUES BASED ACTION

✔	**Prepare:**	*Put a written document together of specific situations to share with Laura where Jason was unfair and disrespectful.*
✔	**Rehearse:**	*Practice with my sister, the HR manager, what I'm going to say to Laura.*
✔	**Execute:**	*Set up the meeting with Laura offsite.*
✔	**Debrief:**	*Discuss with my sister how things went and my next steps.*

HOW THE STORY ENDED
How Margot took charge of the elephant

Margot needed a trusted voice of reason inside the organization, someone who could help her work through this. Margot decided to talk to Jason's boss, Laura. Margot was potentially putting her job on the line, but she knew and trusted Laura, and was fairly certain that Laura was beginning to see through Jason's façade.

Margot had lunch with Laura and told her several stories of how Jason had been disrespectful and unfair. From Laura's perspective, the profile of a completely different Jason began to emerge. Laura had previously sensed that there was something about Jason she didn't quite trust, and given what she was now hearing from Margot, a long-time trusted and proven employee of the company, suggested a leader who was mistreating a valued company asset. Laura realized that Margot needed her help. This could be a personality clash, but she knew Margot to be very personable and sensible. She had had some doubts about Jason before this conversation, but now she really had cause for concern. She thanked Margot for coming in and trusting her with this information and told Margot she'd look into getting her out from under Jason's supervision without exposing their conversation to him. She asked if she'd be willing to work for Susan at the Grand Street office, a satellite office 15 miles away from the corporate office. Susan had been asking for a senior admin due to the increased volume of work they had over there. Margot's eyes lit up and she said she'd love to work for Susan. Laura said she couldn't promise anything yet, but to give her some time to work on it.

A month later Laura met with Jason to tell him more administrative help was needed at the Grand Street office and she wanted to move Margot there as she had trained many of the admins working there now, and her administrative leadership was needed due to the workload they were handling in that office. Always seeking favor with his boss Laura, Jason quickly agreed with her. Laura told Jason that he could work with Brad in Human Resources to find a replacement for Margot.

Within a matter of days Brad was at Laura's door asking if she had a minute, with a concerned look on his face. Laura invited him in and Brad began to share his experience working with Jason for the past few days on finding Margot's replacement. He said in his eleven years as an HR specialist he'd never been treated so rudely and dismissively by an executive. He told Laura that he had tried to talk to Jason about the way he was treating him, and things just got worse when Jason told him he was "getting mighty pushy with a senior executive, and if he knew what was good for him and his career he'd do his job and keep his opinions to himself".

Laura now had what she needed to take disciplinary action with Jason. She prepared herself and called a meeting with Jason and Lynn, the VP of HR and Brad's boss. Jason was told, by both Laura and Lynn, that this was going in his file and that this kind of rude and dismissive behavior from a senior leader would not be tolerated. Any subsequent incidents like this would result in Jason being asked to leave the company.

Four months later, Jason took another job outside the company.

Story 4
The Lonely Road of Integrity
Doing Right When There is No One to Do it but Yourself

> ### *The elephant in the room:*
> *Unethical, illegal, or out-of-policy conduct — visible to many and unaddressed.*

LEARN
THE STORY
THE CRINGE FACTOR LEVEL

Binder felt threatened by his employees and his boss and the HR director. The employees threatened violence if he pursued investigating the theft and his position was undeniably threatened by his boss and the HR director, who were clearly intimidated by the line workers. Binder could think of nothing else and there was a high degree of risk if he pushed this with the employees or his boss and the HR director. Because every attempt had been made to resolve this, he was left with only one option.

		Feeling	Thinking	Risk to Comfort	Options
Cringe Factor	**1**	Bothered	Momentary	Lower	Multiple
	2	Worried	Frequent	Moderate	Narrowing
	3	Anguished	Constant	Elevated	Limited
	4	Threatened	Dominant	High	Singular

$$4 + 4 + 4 + 4 = 16$$
$$16 \div 4 = 4.0 \textbf{ Cringe Factor}$$

EXPLORE
VALUES

Binder felt that *Honesty* alone was not enough as the value at play because he had been honest in the face of dishonesty and it didn't work. He felt *Responsibility* was equally at play because he needed to be the one who was responsible to the company if others weren't upholding their responsibility to the company.

What Binder chose and why:

Honesty	Fairness	Respect	Compassion	Responsibility

Honesty *"Evidence strongly suggested people were being dishonest and committing a crime."*

Responsibility *"My boss and the HR representative are not upholding their responsibility to the company by enforcing company policies."*

ALIGN
VALUES TO OPTIONS

In asking Binder:

Which of these three options align you most with being **honest** and **responsible** toward yourself or others? And what needs to be done to put it in place?

He answered:

☐ Stay and self manage	☒ Address the person directly	☐ Put exit strategy in place
	Honesty *If I were to say or do nothing it would be dishonest — a dishonesty with myself.* **Responsibility** *I am responsible to the company and responsible for upholding company policies.* *The responsible thing to do is to let those in authority know what is happening and to keep trying until I find someone who takes what is happening seriously.*	

DEPLOY
VALUES BASED ACTION

✔ **Prepare:**		*I willl document all the dates, organize the inventory control records showing the discrepancies, create a timeline of events. I also want to get the emotion out of my delivery of this information.*
✔ **Rehearse:**		*I will role play the different ways this can go with my coach until I feel confident.*
✔ **Execute:**		*Have the meeting with Bill at corporate.*
✔ **Debrief:**		*Connect with my coach afterwards to talk through what happens. Talk about future options depending how things go.*

HOW THE STORY ENDED
How Binder took charge and confronted the elephant

Binder and Katherine began to strategize a plan to move forward. While his coach had been selected and hired by Tony and Kara for Binder, Katherine knew that she also had an ethical obligation towards the best interests for Binder and the parent organization, as there was clearly very suspicious activity involved that was being ignored. Katherine asked him if he knew anyone in the company that he trusted, who worked outside of the plant. Binder remembered the former HR director Bill, who was now the VP of HR at the corporate offices. Binder shared that the former HR director had hired him originally and was very supportive, though Binder hadn't had any contact with Bill for several years. Binder was concerned that Bill might not remember him from so long ago. The coach asked if Binder would be willing to contact him regardless. Binder replied, "What do I have to lose?"

Binder called his acquaintance Bill, the VP of HR at the corporate headquarters office, and outlined the entire series of events. Bill requested that Binder email him all of the facts: the timeline, the inventory control records and Binder's attempts to take things further with Tony and Kara. Bill thanked Binder for his perseverance and integrity.

Two days later, a team from the corporate office arrived unannounced, to complete a full audit of the plant. Binder's findings and concerns were confirmed by the audit team, and the nine employees directly responsible for theft were terminated. Binder's manager Tony was placed on a 90-day performance improvement plan and Kara, the director of human resources, was released from employment. Binder was invited to serve on an internal controls team to create improved procedures and processes in the plant.

Eighteen months later, Binder was promoted to assistant plant manager. In his new role, he now teaches an ethics and integrity class for employees once a month.

Chapter 8

7 Strategies to Build Your Courage Muscle

Have you ever seen someone who has mastered being firm yet civil? Direct yet compassionate? Powerful yet authentic? They have the rare ability to speak up, speak out and challenge, without exploding every-thing and everyone. In fact, they seem to have just the opposite effect in that things get done, people fall in line and results happen without anyone being stripped of their dignity or having a piece of their soul ripped out. They wield courage and confidence as if it is part of their DNA and seem to have a different threshold of resilience than most. What do they have that others don't? They place great importance on their own self-awareness and development. They are masters of self-mastery.

Courage is like a muscle. When people put themselves in harm's way in life-threatening situations, they will be the first to say they didn't consider themselves heroes or courageous. They look at their heroic acts as a reflex or reaction to being up against daunting odds and having to do something. Most will say this because they were afraid…often very afraid, in their heroic moment. But somehow they were able to get beyond the fear and act. As Nelson Mandela said, "Courage is not the absence

of fear, but the triumph over it." Sounds great, but how do you attain the internal juice to fuel those courageous acts?

After working with and for some incredibly courageous and resilient leaders, we identified seven strategies anyone can begin to focus on and develop in order to build their resilience and courage. Raising your self-awareness in each area is what gives you the confidence to know what you stand for and against. They will give you the resources to draw from when the going gets tough, and the clarity to know when the tough should get going.

We highly recommend beginning some of this developmental work with a mentor, or VOR as it will keep you accountable to staying focused.

Strategy #1:
Know Your Personal Standards

Personal standards are our personal code of conduct. It's where we set the bar for our behavior, the way we treat others and how we operate personally and professionally. Some examples of personal standards would be:

- I respect other people's time.
- I do what I say I'm going to do.
- I treat others with the same respect as I would like to be treated.

The level at which we hold these standards is as unique as each person. As you can see in the three examples we've used above, there can be large disparities in how two or more people would express those standards — and in those disparities, we have fertile ground for conflict to grow.

Knowing your personal standards builds resilience in that you can quickly identify where you may rub someone the wrong way, and in turn how they may rub you the wrong way. You can rise above it and avoid or work through conflicts by addressing the standard versus a person's character.

One thing Megan could always count on from her boss Wes was that he would be a minimum of ten minutes late for everything. He was notorious for last-minute cancellations too. For the most part Wes was good to work for, but his disrespect for other people's time infuriated Megan. Each time Wes was late, she'd be in such a state of aggravation that she'd be cold and short with him. This dynamic kept the two of them from having a harmonious working relationship. Megan was at a Cringe Factor 3 and respect and fairness were the values in conflict for her.

While talking through how Megan wanted to align with the values in conflict, her wise friend asked her what her personal standards were about respecting other people's time. Megan said she would never disrespect someone else by doing this. She was so careful about this that she always made sure to give herself extra time to get where she needed to be early. Her friend then asked if it was possible her annoyance was about different standards versus Wes being disrespectful. Megan realized that this was in fact just a difference in one standard and that she was ignoring all the other standards they held in common.

By knowing our personal standards, we can move past the assumptions we may have about another person's intentions or their character and see situations for what they are when it's simply a difference in standards.

Strategy #2:
Make Replenishment a Priority Using Your Discretionary Time

Free time is so rare and precious. Because of high stress in leadership roles, how that precious time is used has become littered with soft addictions like overeating, too much TV, excessive internet time, shopping, etc. Discretionary time can also be filled with personal obligations, leaving no time for yourself. When our time is completely full with nothing that refuels our tanks, fatigue and exhaustion set in. Our human bodies were made for short blasts of energy output followed by a period of rest and replenishment. We are biologically wired for this, however, our modern work lives have completely ignored the fact that we can't keep going at full speed without negative effects to our physical and cognitive well-being.

Vince Lombardi once wrote, "Fatigue makes cowards of all of us." Making no time for real replenishment wears down intellectual resiliency and exacerbates tough situations. Confidence and courage take a big hit when we are worn down. Finding your footing and keeping your "self" intact when facing a values conflict is difficult at best and often impossible when you're exhausted. Finding courage is also nearly impossible when you've run the batteries down so low that just getting through the day is all you've got the energy for.

Ben's job required about 70% international travel. When he wasn't traveling he put in long hours at the office. And because he managed teams in Asia, Australia and Europe, he was often waking in the middle of the night for conference calls. Ben never stopped and it was beginning to show. He was about 40 pounds overweight and sorely out of shape. He'd begun to have real trouble with his sleep and couldn't remember the last time he'd slept through the night without waking up at least twice.

Ben was at the end of his tether. He knew if he didn't start making some changes, he might be faced with a serious medical condition that would force him to slow down. He knew his unreasonable boss would never see it from Ben's perspective. The day he did something about it was the day his boss gave Ben hell for not making a meeting in San Antonio. Ben had sent two people from his Dallas office and felt confident things were covered. Ben's boss wasn't happy with that choice and railed at him relentlessly. Ben stood there defenseless, having completely lost the ability to find any words in his own defense. He could feel his ears ringing and his throat going dry. When his boss was done, Ben walked out of the room and his knees buckled and he went down like a limp rag.

After a trip to the ER and a battery of tests, Ben learned he'd had a full-blown panic attack. He also knew he was at a Cringe Factor 4 with his boss and that honesty was the value in conflict. It was Ben's honesty that was in question. He didn't feel he could approach his boss and be honest about the excessive travel and the job being too much for one person without serious consequences that would affect his career. That day in the ER, Ben got serious about how he was going to spend his time moving forward. He stayed home and slept for almost two days straight and when he woke up and went into the office, the first thing he did was ask to be put on his boss's calendar for a meeting. The next day Ben informed his boss that he had to make some changes and that he needed to reduce his travel and delegate some of his responsibilities to some of the high potentials on his team. He told his boss this was non-negotiable because he needed to pay better attention to his health.

Building in time for replenishment is vital to having mental sharpness and acuity which allows for flexibility, buoyancy and resiliency in difficult situations.

Strategy #3:
Surround Yourself with the Right People

We know to surround ourselves with people that lift us up and don't drain our energy in our personal lives. In the workplace we don't get to choose our friends and allies as easily. And yet, we can still OWN our support network and who we choose to emulate and learn from. This can be done by:

- Finding leaders you admire and respect and learn from them
- Keeping a network of past bosses (positive ones!), coaches and mentors that you trust
- Being willing and able to build the muscle to know when and how to distance yourself from the negativity, gossip and dysfunction

Maintaining a good network of both colleagues and friends helps build resiliency. Knowing you have a trusted group that believe in you and that you trust makes tough situations a bit easier to handle.

Diane had a leadership role in the operations organization of a small company that she really enjoyed, but she struggled with the leadership from the president of the company. While the president was a nice person, the leadership changed radically from day to day. There was a lack of consistency in decision making and it often resulted in him asking those under him to "do as I say, not as I do." Diane really liked her co-workers and enjoyed her work but wondered how long she could work for someone that she did not respect. It began to require her to change her leadership style to accommodate requests and to "bite her tongue" at times as to the impact on the organization on some of the decisions the president made. Diane was at a Cringe Factor 2. Fairness and respect were the values in conflict.

Diane had a boss she worked for in her last job that she thought the world of and reached out to him to get a point of view on how to handle this dynamic with her current boss. He had similar experiences in the past with one of his bosses and was able to provide insights on how to handle it without becoming a different person. He provided coaching on how she could still utilize her style that was extremely successful with her team, while meeting her boss's needs as best she could.

In the end, the results would pan out. It turned out that Diane's department performance was above expectations and, over time, the president moved on to another organization. Her new leader was someone she truly respected and she was energized to work for the new leader.

Having a voice of reason to turn to in times of confusion or indecision is invaluable for gaining perspective and insight.

Strategy #4:
Build Reserves

Often what keeps people from taking a courageous stand for their values is a lack of reserves. Because they don't have a reservoir (i.e., more than *just* enough), there is not enough for them to draw on when the cringe moments come that require a personal risk to resolve. Without reserves, it can create a perception that there are no choices or solutions. It can set up a dynamic of feeling victimized, when really there just isn't enough in reserve of something(s) to absorb possible consequences without great difficulty and hardship.

Some key areas to build reserves for courage are:

- Education and training
- An up-to-date resume
- A diverse and up-to-date network
- Financial reserves – six months of living expenses and minimal outstanding credit
- Strong relationships – personal and professional
- Pleasant home environment
- Clutter-free surroundings
- Rest and replenishment
- Change adaptation skills
- Voices of reason and positive influences

Cailyn's Story: Navigating Cringe Moments With Reserves

Cailyn, a credit manager for a mid-size financial institution, had received numerous complaints about the chief financial officer's romantic involvement with an employee who was his direct report. She had personally witnessed the two departing daily for lunch together and had heard the pair speak about shared weekend activities and getting together after work hours. Both individuals were married to others.

The CFO's assistant came to Cailyn stating the CFO had asked her to say he was at an outside business meeting and would be out the rest of the day. There was no business meeting on the CFO's calendar. The assistant was distraught at being asked to lie for her boss. Cailyn knew it was time — she had to speak with the CFO and share the comments she was hearing from others and talk through potential risks for the CFO and the company. She dreaded the conversation and knew she risked getting fired as the CFO was her boss. Cailyn was experiencing a Cringe Factor 4. She identified the values she believed to be compromised were respect and responsibility — for the work team and the organization.

Meeting with the CFO, Cailyn spoke calmly, pointing out the rampant company-wide comments about the CFO and his employee. The CFO vehemently denied an affair was occurring. He stated he and the employee were "just friends." Cailyn invited the CFO to consider actions to minimize the talk in the company. The CFO responded, "I'm changing nothing. We are going to see each other whenever we want." Cailyn left the meeting feeling concerned that this matter would continue to get worse.

Cailyn knew this might not end well for her, but she couldn't remain quiet about the situation as it was affecting others. She had a responsibility to do more, and after a night of looking at her personal finances and exploring her options, she knew she'd be OK for several months if she put her neck on the line and went to the CEO and the corporate attorney, who were both friends outside of work with the CFO. She voiced her concerns to both of them about what was occurring and identified risks to the company and to the CFO. They took a "let's wait and see" position.

Cailyn was at a crossroads. She knew she did not want to work in an environment of disrespect and lack of responsibility. She began searching for her next position outside the company. Three months later, she was in her new position.

Bob's Story: Navigating the Same Cringe Moment Without Reserves

Bob worked in the same department with Cailyn as a financial analyst. He too was aware of the CFO's relationship with one of his direct reports. He felt he had no choice but to keep to himself, even after being asked by the CFO several times to lie to others, namely the CEO and president, by saying they were working on a project together that required late nights.

Bob was experiencing a Cringe Factor 4 just like Cailyn, but he was frozen in fear. Not only was he living month to month financially with a huge amount of credit card debt, he had not built a professional

> *network or kept up with continuing education. He knew he wasn't very marketable for a new job and could not sustain himself and his family financially if something unexpected occurred in his work life.*
>
> *Bob too was at a crossroads; however, he was stuck. He decided to do nothing. It was too scary to rock the boat and felt too risky to take any action at all. He felt awful about being set up to lie on the CFO's behalf but knew he had no choice but to go along with it.*

Reserves sustain and support us when cringe moments occur. Courage lives in partnership with our reserves. They are the life raft to support us in navigating the stormy seas of cringe moments.

Strategy #5:
Yield to Change

> *"Life is 10 percent what happens to you and 90 percent how you respond to it."* — **Lou Holtz**

We are in ever-changing times due to globalization, technological change, economic issues, and the list goes on. Leaders of tomorrow need to be change agents, pure and simple. The more resilient one is to change, the better tooled one will be to "weather the storm" as things change in the workplace. Gone are the days of working for the same company for 30+ years and obtaining a pension. We, and we alone, need to own our careers, our lives and our futures. To do that, there are two types of change that individuals need to be ready for:

1. Changes that happen **to us**.
2. Changes we make **for ourselves** in order to adapt to the changes that happen to us.

Change that happens to us includes: mergers, boss changes, policy changes and organizational changes. For these type of changes, we need to recognize that change is innate and determine how we want to respond to it. We can fight it or yield to it. In some cases, where the change conflicts with our values, we can utilize the LEAD model discussed in this book to determine how big the gap is and how we are going to handle it. Otherwise, there are many models to help organizations with change such as Kotter's model[6] and others that help organizations and people with the change to come.

Changes that we may need to make for ourselves include changing companies, changing careers, changing locations, changing attitudes, changing perspectives and changing limiting beliefs. Far too many times, individuals stay put due to concern over these type of changes and feel stuck and unhappy. It builds courage when you know you have choices in how you want to respond to change versus being victimized by it.

Diane: *Change that Happens to Her*

Diane had been working at her company for 10+ years and was a senior leader in finance. She was leading a project that required a lot of cooperation with the IS team and a new VP IS had been recently announced. Diane was convinced this simply meant more micromanaging on an effort that already had tough deadlines and a lot of work ahead, and frankly she was frustrated she wasn't considered for the role. Diane fretted about the change and was borderline non-inclusive as the new VP came up to speed, since Diane thought the less the new VP was involved, the easier the transition would be for the team. Over a couple of months, the tables began to turn as it turned out that the new VP had a lot of experience in this area and could be a great help to Diane's team, as well as sponsor her career. Over the years, the partnership was of great value to the company and they even became friends. Diane has had numerous boss changes (direct or indirect) since that time of her career. She has learned a lot about how to manage her own reaction, accept that change is a given and develop capability to champion such changes.

---

6   Leading Change by John P. Kotter

Tony: Change He Needed to Own

Tony had worked for his organization for eight years and was at a crossroads. For the past few years, he had been growing increasingly frustrated with the leadership of his department and the company direction was concerning him. Tony plugged along, as he was intensely committed, and hoped things would change. He was not living where he wanted to live and was working for an individual that he did not respect. Tony shared his frustration with his family frequently but did not make simultaneous effort to begin to look at "what's next."

Tony and his boss continued to struggle with trust, collaboration and differing values. Tony knew a family friend that did coaching and, after only a few sessions discussing the situation, learning he had choices in how he could approach and effect change and then scripting conversations with his boss, Tony went on to have a series of open discussions with his boss. They mutually determined a path forward that would benefit both Tony and the organization. Tony felt the weight of the world off his shoulders. He was now going to be able to move to an area where his family and friends were, be more "present" in relationships as he wouldn't be so pre-occupied with a job he hated, and possibly even look at doing something that brought him more joy in his career.

Strategy # 6:
Know Your Blind Spots

Everyone has blind spots. We define blind spots to be unconscious behaviors that cause or invite friction with others. As a result, they create patterns of breakdowns and failures in our personal and professional lives and drive our behavior in ways that we can't see. Ultimately, they don't get us what we want and need. Once we understand our blind spot(s) and how they drive our behavior, we break long-standing cycles of difficulty and free ourselves to move beyond them.

If you're blind to it, how do you see what your blind spot is?

There are two types of blind spots most often seen in leadership. The first type *causes* friction and usually makes others feel wrong, defensive, irritated or angry. Some of those blind spots may be:

- Needing to be right, win, blame or punish
- Insensitivity or lack of awareness to the impact you have on others
- A sense of entitlement (the rules don't apply to you)
- Ambiguous expectations and communication
- Being controlling (driving others into your self-serving agenda)
- Personal filters that you speak and act from which land with others as being insensitive, and make you seem unable to see a different perspective than your own

Deborah could feel her blood pressure rising while the organizational development (OD) consultant read the amalgamated feedback from her 360 assessment, which essentially painted a picture of a control freak. How could this be? She thought she had a very good working relationship with her team and others in the company. The OD consultant went on to say he'd done several personal interviews to get to the core of this pervasive theme in her feedback, and learned most people liked working for and with Deborah; however, when it came to high visibility work that would be seen by the senior leadership team, Deborah went into helicopter-boss mode, hovering over everyone and everything involved. He suggested Deborah work with a coach to understand and turn this dynamic around.

After working with a coach for three months, Deborah began to see ways she was trying to control her people when she felt vulnerable, specifically, when things would be seen by the senior leadership team. Deborah began to understand how her team and others could see her as a control freak. Once acknowledged, Deborah began exploring what was happening when she'd default into controlling behavior. Knowing those triggers helped her to recognize when she felt compelled to become controlling, and with her coach, identified alternative behaviors for her to use. This allowed her to interact with her team and others in a way that built deeper connections and catalyzed higher performance.

The other type of blind spot *invites* friction and usually opens the door for others to take advantage, undermine or overpower. Some of those blind spots may be:

- Wanting to be liked by everyone
- Avoiding conflict
- Not holding others accountable
- Needing approval
- Feeling responsible for *everything*

Kristin stormed into Daniel's office waving a piece of paper and plunked it down on his desk saying, "That's it, Daniel! I'm no longer willing to have my team work another weekend because your people aren't hitting the target dates we all agreed on!" Daniel looked down and saw several red boxes in the project timeline, all of them in his area. He looked up and apologized to Kristin. He knew his team was falling behind on their deadline dates and he vowed to make it up to Kristin. Kristin then delivered a hard message to hear, but he needed to hear it. She told Daniel that his team loved him and that was great; however, they loved him because he never held any of them accountable and often made excuses for them when they didn't deliver. Daniel vowed to get things back on track. His boss had put an identical message in his performance review last month and offered to support Daniel in growing as a more assertive leader. He knew he needed to do something.

Daniel took his boss up on the offer and hired a coach to help him develop some "tough love" skills. He learned that he could be tough and civil at the same time. This helped Daniel be more assertive as a leader in general and also got him more visibility from senior leadership.

Knowing we can enter into Cringe Moments without getting blindsided by our own self-sabotaging behavior boosts confidence greatly to enter into situations that require courage.

Strategy #7:
Stop Putting up with So Much

We all have unpleasant conditions in our lives that cause us stress. We may try to ignore these situations, but they still affect us. If the condition CAN be eliminated, it is called a ***toleration.***

What is a toleration? It's the handle that is missing off the bottom drawer of your desk and you just haven't had time to call maintenance in to fix it. It's the fluorescent light that flickers outside your office door causing numerous headaches in the past few weeks or the stapler that jams every time you use it.

A toleration is something that we put up with or endure; it is a burden and eats up time, money, and mental space. We may complain about the toleration to others, yet do nothing about it. Other examples of tolerations include:

- A desk stacked with paper
- A co-worker who spends all day complaining
- The boss who isn't clear with his expectations of you
- A human resources department that sends you unqualified candidates to hire

Tolerations can be significantly reduced or eliminated altogether. The desk full of paper can be organized, you can stop listening to your co-worker complain, you ask your boss for a clear set of objectives and his expectations of you relative to those objectives, and you can request that HR follow your specific guidelines on who you want to hire before interviewing.

It is important to note that one person's toleration is another person's way of life. A messy desk may bother you and not bother someone else in the least. Like personal standards, tolerations can vary greatly from person to person and can also be a source of tension between people. Basically, it's a toleration for you if it creates frustration, drains your energy, or distracts you from what is really important.

What are the benefits of identifying and eliminating your tolerations:

- Reduced frustration and anxiety
- More energy
- More freedom

More than anything, Mateo wanted to move up in the high-tech company where he worked. He considered himself to be a loyal employee for the past five years. His first position at the company was a system engineer. He loved the work and learned a lot during the first two years. He recently had seen a job posting for a network manager. Mateo viewed this position as a dream job. He was eager to apply for the position.

Mateo spoke with his current supervisor. While the supervisor wanted to support Mateo, she reminded him of performance issues in his last review. Those included incomplete tasks, sloppy appearance when meeting with clients, inability to find electronic files due to an over-cluttered hard drive and excessive complaining to others about his work load. She reminded him that these concerns were within his control to change. She advised Mateo that the tolerations might impact the interview process for the open position. Mateo agreed that he needed to refocus on the tolerations impacting his performance and said that he wanted to apply for the position anyway and see what evolved.

Mateo began searching for his resume in his electronic files. He noticed his files had grown to over 3,500 files on his hard drive. After two hours, he abandoned the search and went to the human resources department to see if they had a copy of the resume he had submitted when he first started work at the company. He discovered the human resources department was going through a software upgrade and would not have access to employee files for a week.

He returned to his office frustrated that he had allowed his lack of organization to reach this level. He hammered out a quick resume and submitted it for the new position.

Mateo did not get the position. The hastily produced resume had misspellings and omissions of his education credentials and certifications. Mateo was very disappointed in not getting the promotion. He vowed to create a Tolerations List to better manage his life.

Chapter 9

Summing Things Up

We have captured the most important concepts in this book in visuals for quick reference and deeper understanding.

> **You are the boss of YOU.**
>
> *No one can take away your ability to make choices that align with your values. Doing so is what keeps you leading with integrity.*

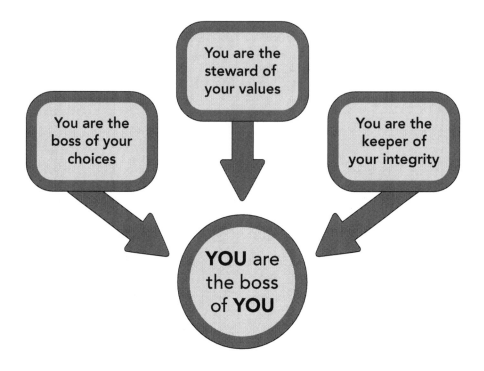

If you are experiencing a Cringe Moment Conundrum, you are not alone.

Studies show power dynamics including incivility, contentious politics and bullying exist in almost every organization.

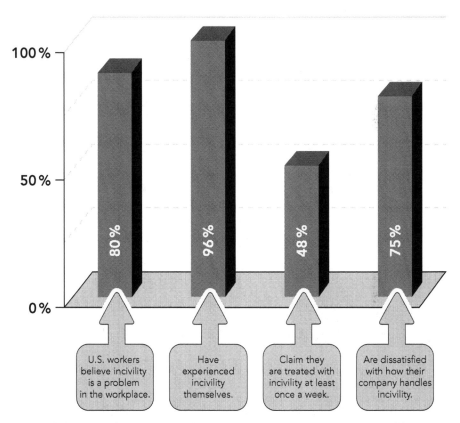

(The Cost of Bad Behavior by Christine Pearson & Christine Porath)

Disengagement and trust break down one Cringe Moment at a time.

It is imperative that leaders model self-awareness and commitment to values when handling Cringe Moments.

Is it me?	Is it them?	Is it us?	Is it the organization?
• Others aren't reacting in the same way • Same patterns in your past	• Others are reacting in the same way • Breach of ethics, policies or law	• Communication style • Work standards • Personality type	• Special treatment • Unclear policies • Mixed message of rewards vs company values • Incentivize results over behavior

There is a way to find resolution in even the most egregious situations.

RESOLUTION

> ### As the Cringe Factor Level increases, the ability to reason soundly decreases.
> *Options also typically decrease, you become smaller and the situation looms larger as it becomes all-consuming.*

Cringe Factor		Feeling	Thinking	Risk to Comfort	Options
	1	Bothered	Momentary	Lower	Multiple
	2	Worried	Frequent	Moderate	Narrowing
	3	Anguished	Constant	Elevated	Limited
	4	Threatened	Dominant	High	Singular

Cringe Factor Level Feelings

4
Threatened, panicked,
afraid, unsafe, intimidated, exposed,
vulnerable, jeopardized, unprotected, overwhelmed,
at risk, attacked, bullied, coerced, pressured, denounced

3
Anguished, despair, miserable,
strained, overcome, stewing, agonizing, suffering,
dejected, oppressed, pained, tormented, crushed,
troubled, humiliation, mistreated, exploited, offended

2
Worried, upset, distressed, bad vibes, flustered,
apprehensive, on edge, suspicious, upset, stunned,
mistrustful, troubled, uncertain, tense, uneasy, alarmed,
shaken, judged

1
Bothered, discouraged,
marginalized, distracted, concerned, agitated,
provoked, unbalanced, irked, frustrated,
annoyed, bugged, undermined, rattled, insulted,
disappointed, confused, misled

Finding a VOR (Voice of Reason)

It's helpful to have one at any Cringe Factor Level and recommended for Levels 3 & 4

Qualities to look for in a VOR
- Emotionally mature
- Seasoned
- Impartial and objective
- Honest and supportive
- Drama-free zone
- Firm, articulate and compassionate
- Resourceful

Identifying the Values at Play

We all share five distinct values that are directly connected to our moral compass and sense of right and wrong. They are the filter for decision making. Aligning values with choices and actions is what moves you forward with your integrity intact.

Fairness	
When fairness is upheld you will experience:	**When fairness is in jeopardy you will experience:**
Civility	Marginalization
Decency	Lack of consistency
Tolerance	Rudeness
Honor	Injustice
Justice	Partiality
Reasonable	Favoritism
Give-and-take	Biased
Open mindedness	Unilateral decisions

Honesty	
When honesty is upheld you will experience:	**When honesty is in jeopardy you will experience:**
Candor	Lying
Frankness	Dishonesty
Genuine	Uninterested
Loyalty	Embellishment
Morality	Disloyalty
Sincerity	Immorality
Virtue	Cheating
Conscientiousness	Fraudulent behavior
Authenticity	Deception
Principled	

Compassion

When compassion is upheld you will experience:	When compassion is in jeopardy you will experience:
Benevolence	Animosity
Empathy	Cruelty
Humaneness	Ill Will
Kindness	Meanness
Sympathy	Mercilessness
Responsiveness	Harshness
Concern	Indifference
	Apathy
	Coldness

Respect

When respect is upheld you will experience:	When respect is in jeopardy you will experience:
Appreciation	Excessive criticism
Considerate behavior	Disdain
Honoring of dignity	Disregard
Regards wishes	Disrespect
Recognition	Ignore
Courteousness	Neglectfulness
Acknowledgement	Disfavor
	Thoughtlessness

Responsibility

When responsibility is upheld you will experience:	When responsibility is in jeopardy you will experience:
Accountability	Blamelessness
Commitment	Irresponsibility
Answerable	Unreliable
Prioritized	Untrustworthy
Engagement	Self-serving
Obligation	Self-exempted
Duty-bound	Immunity

> **Courage is like a muscle and needs to be built.**
>
> *There are seven strategies anyone can begin to focus on and develop in order to build their resilience and courage.*

**Personal
Standards**

**Discretionary
Time**

**Yield to
Change**

**Know Your
Blind Spots**

**Build
Reserves**

**Reduce
Tolerations**

**Have the
Right People**

The Last Word......

You will never be perfect at this. People dynamics are a messy business. Being 100% certain and without fear while navigating Cringe Moment Conundrums usually means you wouldn't have a conscience. Even the strongest leaders who appear to have the greatest leadership talents struggle in these power dynamics. It's how you handle them that makes the difference. The two things strong leaders who lead with integrity have in common are:

1. A good night's sleep
2. A clean rearview mirror.

They sleep well at night knowing they did the best they could for the right reasons. And when they look back at what they have done and accomplished as leaders, they see a path walked in alignment with their values and guided by integrity.

And last, coming to resolution with a Cringe Moment Conundrum takes time. This is, by no means, an overnight process. Sometimes it takes weeks or even months to play out. Knowing you are actually doing *something* can make all the difference. A difference of living a "life of quiet desperation" or being empowered in knowing YOU are the boss of YOU.

Chapter 10

How We Can Help You
The Shameless Plug

INTEGRESHIP. COM

What is Integreship_{SM}?

Integreship_{SM} is an amalgamation of essential traits strong and highly effective leaders possess which we've coined into one word. Traits that are not easy to live by, yet without them can lead us to a slippery slope when faced with difficult decisions and conflicting interests.

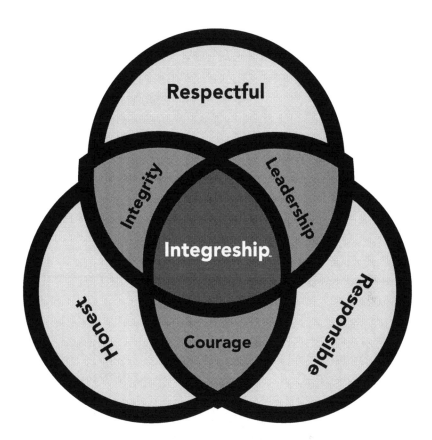

Leaders are not born into **Integreship**ₛₘ, instead they choose it day by day, in each decision they make and the multitude of interactions they have. And for every time a leader chooses **Integreship**ₛₘ, they develop a stronger resilience and muscle for the realities of leadership.

Let's face it, we have a leadership crisis. With the business climate today we are hungry for leaders who are tough but civil. Fiercely committed, yet fair. Quietly determined but courageous in doing what needs to be done and saying what needs to be said. Instead, we have leaders who, for the most part, are just trying to keep up. They are faced with near-impossible objectives that demand they forge on without looking back at the collateral damage. They're asked to dance, almost flawless-ly, through a gauntlet of competing priorities. Unremittingly trying to strike an impossible balance between the needs of stakeholders and the countless conflicting needs of their employees. They face unrelent-ing pressure to keep people scores high and stakeholders quiet and happy. This constant tension has set many leaders up to fail miserably at being decent human beings. These are the realities of leadership.

Despite $15 billion plus being spent each year on leadership development by U.S. companies, there is still something missing. But what?

The **Integreship**₍ₛₘ₎**Group** may have the answer. We are proposing a new approach to developing leaders. **Our mission is to provide on-demand leadership support and development…with a twist.**

We focus on the tough stuff.

- Contentious politics
- Bullying
- Incivility
- Power struggles

- Difficult feedback
- Personality clashes
- Communication breakdowns
- …… and much more

We provide just-in-time support for leaders facing those realities of leadership that become moments of truth.

We believe most leaders are good people who lack the support and resources to lead with **Integreship**₍ₛₘ₎. We also believe leaders can be developed to do so with just-in-time support that provides tools, coaching, mentoring and learning resources that will help them navigate those tough realities when they happen.

*Services from The Integreship*ₛₘ*Group*

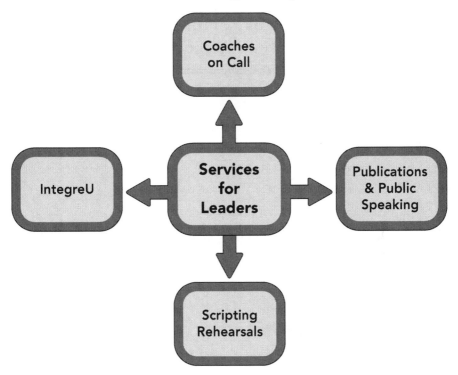

Coaches on Call

Immediate access to professionally trained executive coaches who are also seasoned leaders. Coaching is brief and targeted to help leaders navigate and resolve tough spots. Only one to three sessions are usually required to get to a resolution and plan to move forward.

Publications & Speaking

Books and social media filled with resources and tools for leaders to navigate the tough stuff. Public speaking on a variety of topics related to **Integreship**ₛₘ.

IntegreU

An on-demand, interactive multi-media eLibrary with a two-pronged approach to leadership development, which focuses on navigating complex power dynamics:

1. *Leaders to Learn From*: On-demand virtual modules that capture seasoned leaders sharing their experiences, what they learned from them and how it impacted their success.
2. *Self-Mastery Modules*: A unique collection of skills and resources from a wide variety of experts that contribute to the inner and outer growth of a leader. The stuff that builds character and grit and shifts thinking and behavior from being "the boss" to being a leader.

Scripting Rehearsals

A virtual learning lab utilizing cutting-edge technology, where leaders receive individual coaching and mentoring on messaging, delivery, language and influencing from some of the best coaches in the business, who are also seasoned leaders themselves.

Who We Work With

Individual Leaders

Leaders who are stuck and struggling in a power dynamic and are seeking just-in-time support to manage complex or potentially volatile situations.

Teams and Organizations

For companies seeking to provide internal leaders with just-in-time support, we provide corporate accounts in the following ways:

- Batch purchase of coaching hours
- Multi-user subscriptions to IntegreU virtual learning modules (available Jun 2016)
- Batch purchase of Scripting (Cringe Moment) Rehearsals and Cringe Moment Bootcamp
- OD systems consulting for company-wide initiatives

Visit Our Website for Resources to Supplement This Book

We will be continually adding to resources to supplement your learning from this book. There you'll find:

- Access to some of the best coaches in the business with **Coaches on Call**. Coaching from seasoned leaders on your Cringe Moment. The coaching is brief (one to three sessions) and laser-focused to get you through a tough situation. There is no long-term commitment, just as much as you need to get you through your situation.
  » **www.Integreship.com/coaches-on-call**

- **Who's the Boss Workbook** which will provide worksheets to help guide you, or for you to guide someone else, through navigating a Cringe Moment.
  » **www.Integreship.com/WTB-resources**

- **Videos and Podcasts** showcasing real leaders addressing specific concepts from this book and other leadership conundrums.
  » **www.Integreship.com/leaders-to-learn-from**

- **Video Rehearsals and Coaching** to help you script your Cringe Moment conversation and help you develop your Courage Muscle.
  » **www.Integreship.com/cringe-moment-rehearsals**

- **Robust social media** on Twitter (@LEADwCourage), FaceBook (Facebook.com/Integreship), LinkedIn (The Integreship Group)
  » **www.Integreship.com**

- **Demonstrations on how to coach** someone through a Cringe Moment.
  » **www.Integreship.com/IntegreU**

- **Self-Mastery** learning from seasoned leaders to build your courage muscle.
  » **www.Integreship.com/Self-Mastery-Modules**

As we said in the beginning of this book, this is just the beginning of the conversation about leading with integrity. We are committed to making leadership honorable and revered once again, where we put up our brightest and best to lead the way for others, with courage and integrity.

62857799R00060

Made in the USA
Lexington, KY
20 April 2017